Landscapes of
IBIZA
and Formentera

a countryside guide
Fourth edition

Hans Losse

SUNFLOWER BOOKS

For my daughter Angelika

Fourth edition © 2014
Sunflower Books™
PO Box 36160
London SW7 3WS, UK
www.sunflowerbooks.co.uk

ISBN 978-1-85691-436-9

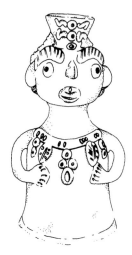

The Punic goddess Tanit

Important note to the reader

We have tried to ensure that the descriptions and maps in this book are error-free at press date. The book will be updated, where necessary, whenever future printings permit. It will be very helpful for us to receive your comments (sent in care of the publishers, please) for the updating of future printings.

We also rely on those who use this book — especially walkers — to take along a good supply of common sense when they explore. Conditions change fairly rapidly on Ibiza and Formentera, and *storm damage or bulldozing may make a route unsafe at any time*. If the route is not as we outline it here, and your way ahead is not secure, return to the point of departure. *Never attempt to complete a tour or walk under hazardous conditions!* Please read carefully the notes on pages 8-15, the Country code on page 17, and the introductory comments at the beginning of each tour and walk (regarding road conditions, equipment, grade, distances and time, etc). Explore *safely*, while at the same time respecting the beauty of the countryside.

If you would like to offset the carbon dioxide emissions for your trip to the Balearic Islands, go to www.climatecare.org.

Cover photograph: Es Vedrà
Title page: Eivissa from the sea

Photographs: the author, except for the cover: shutterstock
Maps: Sunflower Books, updated from the *Mapa Topográfico Nacional de España*; Ibiza in 9 sheets, scale 1:25,000
Drawings by John Theasby
A CIP catalogue record for this book is available from the British Library.
Printed and bound in England: Short Run Press

10 9 8 7 6 5 4 3 2 1

Contents

3

❋ Preface

Up until about 1960, Ibiza belonged to the Ibizans, and only a few artists, poets and writers lived in this paradise. In the 60s the flower-children arrived, hippies and drop-outs. Since then mass tourism has taken over and unfortunately destroyed much of the charm of Ibiza and Formentera.

But not everything on the islands has been spoiled. 'Bed and burgerbar' building reached saturation point years ago, and a visit to the 'pine islands' (the 'Pityussae', as the Greeks called them) is still worthwhile today. There's an unending wealth of hidden beauty spots to be discovered, and I hope that this new edition of the book helps you to find the best of Ibiza and Formentera, whether you travel by car, bicycle, or on foot.

Set off on Ibiza with a hired car or by coach, to get an overview. On Formentera, always get about by bike! Then take one or two short walks, or go for a picnic in one of the beautiful countryside settings suggested on pages 111 to 113. Later, when you're a little more familiar with the terrain, why not try a longer walk or cycle tour? On hot summer days, it's best to stick to the coast, where there's always a pleasant breeze. On cloudy days, however, it's not too hot to try an inland walk. When you're walking along the coast, you'll come upon many splendid beaches and coves — and walking and cycling are always more pleasant after a refreshing swim.

'You've only ever been somewhere, if you've been there on foot' is a wise old saying. Test the truth of this maxim yourself, and get to know the Ibiza and Formentera most tourists miss!

Acknowledgements
Thanks to all my friends and companions who joined me on the walks and cycle tours; Señora Neus Tur and Señora Carmen Sanchez from Ibiza Travel, who supported my work in so many ways; John Theasby for his drawings; my publisher, Pat Underwood, for her encouragement over the years.

Place names
Place names on all the Balearic Islands are changing to the local dialect (Ibicenco in the case of Ibiza), and you will find many different spellings in use. In this book we have used the spellings most common on island signposting.

Touring

Ibiza is a small island — only about 40 kilometres long by 25 kilometres wide (25 by 15.5 miles). By car you'll need hardly more than an hour to go from one end of the island to the other. Even by bus you can get to almost every village in the summer.

The car touring notes are very brief. They include little history or other information that you can obtain in general guides — or free at tourist information offices. For the same reason, the 'sights' of the towns are not described either. I've concentrated instead on the 'logistics' of touring: times and distances, road conditions, and taking you to places many tourists miss. Most of all, the car tours highlight opportunities for **walking** and **picnicking**.

The three car tours begin and end in Eivissa (Ibiza Town). If you do all three drives — including the

detours — you'll have a very good overview of all the island's landscapes.

The fold-out touring map is designed to be held out opposite the touring notes and contains all the information you will need outside the towns. Plans of Sant Antoni, Santa Eulària and Eivissa are on pages 20-23. All distances are *cumulative kilometres* from Eivissa. The **symbols** used in the touring notes correspond to those on the touring map; see map key for clarification.

Drive slowly and carefully. In the high season the traffic is heavy and, since distances are short, there's no need to drive fast. **Petrol stations** are numerous in the towns and on the main roads. **Hire cars** are available at many places, but it is usually cheaper to pre-book before you go. Do check out the car before you take it on the road, make sure you're aware of all the conditions in the car insurance, and carry the hire firm's telephone number with you at all times — including a number where they can be contacted outside opening hours.

Almond blossom near Santa Agnès (Car tour 3, Walk 13)

☀ Walking

Most of the walks described in this book follow coastal tracks and paths. There's always a cool breeze blowing near the coast, and this means that you can walk even in high summer.

If you're fairly fit, you'll find all walks on Ibiza easy. You don't have to be an experienced hiker to get to know this island on foot. Only three walks (Walks 4, 13 and 15) require really careful footwork. But note that in some cases paths are overgrown, making for uncomfortable going. It would be best if novice walkers avoided these overgrown paths.

Before you start a walk please read the complete description carefully and take a look at the map. Try to keep the important landmarks in mind. And remember: names of houses and restaurants may change, or a path may become private. If you have the various landmarks fixed in your mind, you won't go wrong.

Beginners might look at pages 111-113, where they will find a large selection of generally easy walks to picnic spots.

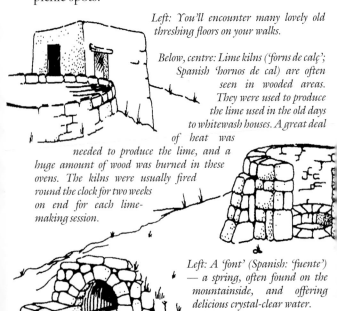

Left: You'll encounter many lovely old threshing floors on your walks.

Below, centre: Lime kilns ('forns de calç'; Spanish 'hornos de cal) are often seen in wooded areas. They were used to produce the lime used in the old days to whitewash houses. A great deal of heat was needed to produce the lime, and a huge amount of wood was burned in these ovens. The kilns were usually fired round the clock for two weeks on end for each lime-making session.

Left: A 'font' (Spanish: 'fuente') — a spring, often found on the mountainside, and offering delicious crystal-clear water.

Waymarking and maps

Some of the walks are **waymarked**. Among the many colours, there are very old red dots, painted by Ibicencos for Ibicencos, when the only way to cross the island was on foot. Coloured metal poles and wooden fingerposts for mountain bikers have been set up over the last two decades by the island tourist board. On some walks you'll find green/white stripes, on others pale blue dots or arrows, painted by landowners to divert walkers round their properties. But the most important waymarks are the dark blue triangles originally painted by a German walking guide who lived on Ibiza and still maintained today. While waymarks are very helpful, remember that my walks may not *always* follow the waymarks, *so please read the text carefully.*

For all the walks described here, the **maps** printed in the book (scale 1:40,000) should be adequate. They have been adapted from the 1:25,000 *Mapa topográfico Nacional de España* set published by the National Geographical Institute of Spain. You can buy these maps on the island or order them in advance from your usual map supplier. The set is comprised of nine sheets and is quite up-to-date — despite the latest edition having been published over ten years ago (Second edition, 2002).

Right: 'Talaias' (Spanish: 'talayas, atalayas') are ancient watchtowers, built in the 16th century as protection against pirates and Turkish invaders. You'll see these towers on all exposed coastal points on both Ibiza and Formentera. From these watchtowers enemy ships were spotted when still far off the coast, allowing ample time for the alarm to be raised. Since the towers were built within sight of each other, warnings could be conveyed from one to another (using flares). The community at risk could then take shelter in another type of tower — a defence tower, like the one shown on page 27.

Sometimes a door closes off the entrance to the 'font'.

What to take with you

For all the walks in this book you need only lightweight walking gear. Light shoes are sufficient for most of the coastal paths, provided that you have rubber soles with good grip. But far better are lightweight walking boots that cover your ankles; a sprained or even broken ankle is not only very painful, but will put paid to your walking holiday.

A long-sleeved shirt should be worn at least on your first couple of walks, so that you don't burn your arms. And of course, *always wear a sunhat*. What's good for the arms holds true for your legs. Only walk in shorts after your legs are very well sun-tanned. Long trousers are also mandatory on overgrown paths. Always take bathing gear and sunglasses with you on coastal walks. Outside the summer months you also need lightweight rainwear, an anorak, and a fleece.

A 1-litre water container should always be in your small rucksack … as should sun cream, insect repellent and a small first-aid kit. You never know when a torch or whistle will come in handy, and a mobile phone will help you summon a taxi — or help in emergencies (the emergency number is 112).

Be sure to take extra food and drink on longer walks!

Where to stay

If you're planning to do a lot of walking, it's best to stay in **Eivissa (Ibiza Town)**, since the bus network radiates from the capital and buses leave for all parts of the island each morning. **Santa Eulària** and **Sant**

Left: charcoal-burning places ('sitjas') are circular mounds of earth, usually edged with stones. These are all that remains today of the old charcoal-burning industry. Here (as in the case of the lime kilns described on page 8) fires burned round the clock. Usually the charcoal-burner lived with his family in a hut near the 'sitja'. You'll become familiar with much of Ibiza's past on your walks. For instance, you'll come across many lovely old wells like the one shown on the left (see also the photograph on page 103), and you are likely to see old stone bread-ovens ('forns de pan') like the one on the right.

Antoni are also good bases. In fact any resort is suitable if it has a morning bus departure. Of course, if you hire a car, you have far more flexibility. Two other good ways of accessing walks on this relatively small island are the coastal boat services (see page 131) and by bike: the free 'Cyclotourist' guide available from tourist offices shows 23 waymarked cycling routes. Leave your bike *(locked!)* in a safe place and do a walk or part of a walk.

Climate and weather
The climate on Ibiza (and Formentera) is suitable for year-round walking. The months of November, December and January could be quite rainy, but even in winter it is very rare for the temperature to fall below freezing. Likewise, in August is it very rare for the temperature to rise above 30°C.

If you don't mind the strong winds in October and February, you can walk on both islands from the beginning of February until the end of October. In July and August, however, only walk along the coast.

You can reckon on sunshine 300 days of the year and good swimming from May until November.

Dogs and other things that bite
On your walks you will pass many *fincas* (farms), and these always have watchdogs. They are mostly chained up. Should you come upon an unchained and aggressive **dog**, you can keep him at bay with a walking stick or by picking up a stone. But never threaten a friendly dog in this manner. If you would like to invest in an ultrasonic 'Dog Dazer', they are for sale on the web. Always carry **insect repellent** as part of the small first-aid kit in your rucksack. In 2011 **snakes** were brought to the islands with trees imported from the mainland, so take special care before resting your hand on a drystone wall and use a stout stick to thump the ground before sitting down. There are *no* **scorpions** or other nasties around.

Spanish for walkers
On Ibiza and Formentera both Spanish and the Ibizenc dialect are spoken. You won't need to learn any Ibizenc, but it's always good to have a few words of Spanish at your disposal — both for greeting people and for asking the way, should you get lost. A little pocket phrase book is of course a good investment.

Here's an (almost) foolproof way to communicate in Spanish. First, memorise the few short key questions and their possible answers, given below. Then, when you have your 'mini-speech' memorised, always ask the many questions you can concoct from it in such a way that you get a 'sí' (yes) or 'no' answer. *Never* ask an open-ended question like 'Where is the main road?' Instead, ask the question and then *suggest the most likely answer yourself.* For instance: 'Good day, sir. Please. Where is the path to Cala Llonga? Is it straight ahead?' Now, unless you get a 'sí' response, try: 'Is it to the left?' If you go through the list of answers to your own question, you will eventually get a 'sí' response — probably accompanied by a vigorous nod of the head.

Below are the three most likely situations in which you may have to practice your Spanish. The dots (…) show where you fill in the name of your destination. Ask locally for help in pronouncing place names.

Asking the way
The key questions

English	Spanish	Pronunciation
Good day,	Buenos días,	Boo-**ay**-nos **dee**-ahs,
sir (madam, miss).	señor (señora, (señorita).	sayn-**yor** (sayn-**yo**-rah, (sayn-yo-**ree**-tah).
Please —	Por favor —	Por fa-**vor** —
Where is	Dónde está	**Don**-day es-**tah**
the road to …?	la carretera a …?	la kar-ray-**tay**-rah ah …?
the path to …?	la senda de …?	la **sen**-dah day …?
the track to …?	el camino a …?	el kah-**mee**-noh ah …?
the bus stop?	la parada?	la pah-**rah**-dah?
Many thanks.	Muchas gracias.	**Moo**-chas **gra**-thee-as.

Possible Answers

English	Spanish	Pronunciation
Is it here?	Está aquí?	Es-**tah** ah-**key**?
there	allá?	ahl-**yah**?
straight ahead?	todo recto?	**toh**-doh rayk-toh?
behind?	detrás?	day-**trahs**?
to the right?	a la derecha?	ah lah day-**ray**-tscha?
to the left?	a la izquierda?	ah lah ith-key-**ayr**-dah?
above?	arriba?	ah-**ree**-bah?
below?	abajo?	ah-**bah**-hoh?

Asking a taxi driver to take you somewhere and return

English	Spanish	Pronunciation
Please —	Por favor —	Por fa-**vor** —
Would you take us to …	Llévanos a …	**L-yay**-va-nohs ah …
Collect us again at (place) at (time).*	Venga buscarnos a … a … *.	**Vayn**-gah bus-**kar**-nohs ah (…) ah (…)*.

*Just point to the time on your watch

Meeting a landowner who denies you access

English	Spanish	Pronunciation
We are going to …	Nos vamos a …	Nos **va**-mos a …
If this route	Si este camino	Si **es**-tay ka-**mee**-noh
is private,	es privado,	es pree-**va**-doh,
please —	por favor —	por fa-**vor** —
show us the	muéstranos	mo-**ays**-tra-nos
correct way.	el camino.	ayl ka-**mee**-noh.
Many thanks.	Muchas gracias.	**Moo**-chas **gra**-thee-as.

Organisation of the walks

The walks (and cycle tours) in this book are based on Eivissa (Ibiza Town), Sant Antoni, and the resorts around Santa Eulària (including Es Figueral, Can Jordi, Es Canar). The general area of each walk is shown on the pull-out touring map. Quickly flipping through the book, you will see that there's at least one photograph for each walk.

Having selected one or two potential excursions based on the map and the photographs, turn to the relevant walk. At the top of the page you'll find planning information: times and distances, grade, equipment, and how to get there and return by public transport (see timetables on pages 131-134). Note also that there are short versions of several walks, especially suitable for beginners, those of you with children, or on hot days.

When you are on your walk, you will find that the text begins with an introduction and then quickly turns to a detailed description of the route itself. The large-scale maps (all reproduced at 1:40,000) have been specially annotated for use in conjunction with the text.

Walking times vary so greatly that I would suggest you compare your pace with mine on one or two short walks, before you set off on a longer hike. Only short stops for photography and waiting for laggards to catch up are included. Make allowances for protracted stops.

Below is a key to the symbols used on the walking maps.

dual carriageway	●▸ spring, etc		🗗	watch/defense tower
main road	— 400 — height in metres		■	castle, fort
secondary road	✝✝ church.chapel		Π	ancient site
minor road	† shrine or cross		■	specified building
track (some may be motorable)	⊞ cemetery		✕	quarry, mine
path, narrow trail	🕮 best views		▤	sports ground
main walk	🚍 bus stop		●	*sitja*, threshing floor
alternative walk	⚓ ferry point		⦂	steep drops!
cycling route	🚗 car parking		◠◠	cliffs
	P good picnic spot		⛕	map continuation

✺ Cycling

The cycle tours described for both islands are shown on the pull-out maps at the back of the book. If you're keen on cycling on **Ibiza**, probably the most useful map is the Kompass map of Ibiza and Formentera (1:50,000). However, for **Formentera** I strongly recommend that you buy the large-scale (1:25,000) *Mapa de Formentera* that is sold in many supermarkets, kiosks and book-shops. In addition to its larger scale, it contains a lot of useful information. You could put whichever map you are using in a clear plastic envelope and secure it to the handlebars, so that it's handy for easy reference.

On Ibiza my tours follow mostly quiet country roads or lanes. On Formentera, the cyclists' paradise, there are cycle paths on both sides of the main motor roads, marked off by white lines. You can cycle two abreast here without danger. But, unfortunately, there is no cycle path on the steep section up to the Mola plateau.

R oads and tracks

Note that in this book only the main roads are printed in red; other asphalted roads and lanes are shown in yellow. Tracks are shown as solid black lines, although many of them will be wide, motorable tracks. Most of the cycle touring routes on Ibiza are also shown on the walking maps in far greater detail.

If you use the large-scale *Mapa de Formentera* referred to above, note that the roads shown in red are asphalted, as they are in this book. Country lanes, only *some* of which are asphalted, are printed in dark green. Most of the time you can cycle easily on these country lanes, but sometimes you will have to push your bike.

Only bits and pieces of the old main road across the island (the 'Camí Vell de la Mola') are still to be found. Parts of this old mule track are asphalted; other bits are so rough that you'll have to get off and push the bike.

E quipment and clothing

If you're not cycling in the middle of winter, wear shorts. Be sure to wear something on your head in high summer. Sunglasses, too, are a must: they not only protect your eyes from the ultraviolet rays, but from dust and insects as well. Be sure to carry the telephone number of the cycle rental firm, and arrange in advance that they will come and fetch you if you have a break-down anywhere on the island, whether Ibiza or Formentera. Of course a bicycle lock is mandatory; when you go to the beach, you'll be leaving the bike far out of sight, in the shade of trees. Finally, you must carry a bicycle pump. These are almost impossible to buy on the islands; your hire firm should supply you with one.

Climate and weather

You can cycle on Ibiza and Formentera all year round. It's not too hot even in July and August; sea breezes — and the breeze you create yourself when cycling — keep you pleasantly cool. In winter, you're likely to have the islands all to yourself, but be sure to take warmer clothing with you, including raingear.

Organisation of the cycle tours

Bicycle hire in available in all the tourist centres; it summer it costs about 10 € a day. Some hotels keep bicycles and give them free to their guests. Plan your daily excursions carefully: my tour descriptions only include the total number of kilometres (miles) that you will travel, and cycling times vary greatly. The cycles for hire on the islands have no odometers. Allow for an average speed of between 8-12 km/h (5-7 mph).

Make sure that the hire firm adjusts the saddle and handlebars for you before you set off (or do it yourself); if the adjustments are not correct, you will tire quickly.

Cycling enthusiasts may wish to take their own bikes to the islands with them. If you're going to stay for any length of time, this is a good idea. It's possible: get details from your travel agent.

The distances quoted are *cumulative* kilometres from the starting point of the tour. But where the capital letters KM *precede a distance* (as in KM5), this refers to a specific *kilometre marker stone* on the road. So, for example, KM4.5 means about half-way between the 4 and 5 kilometre marker stones.

Both islands have waymarked cycling routes, with signposts giving the names of the trails and their length. On Ibiza there are routes off all descriptions, from easy to very strenuous mountain biking trails; on Formentera most routes are easy to moderate. The tourist offices can give you brochures about all these trails.

Picnicking

The picnic spots suggested on pages 111-113 lie along the walks in this book and have been chosen for their fine views. Most are easily reached after a short walk

from the nearest village; a few involve some climbing. The walking time to the picnic spot is shown in **bold type**.

Picnic numbers correspond to walk numbers (or, on Formentera, to cycle tour numbers). You can quickly find the general location of Ibiza picnics by referring to the Ibiza touring map, where walk areas are shown. The exact location of the picnic spot is shown on the corresponding *walking* map (for Formentera on the *cycling* map) by the letter *P*, printed in green. If you are feeling lazy, in some cases you can drive even closer to the picnic spot by using these large-scale walking and cycling maps. But these picnic suggestions are chiefly intended to encourage you to stretch your legs on some short walks.

Remember to look over the comments at the start of the relevant walk before you set off for your picnic; if a fairly long walk is involved, remember to wear stout shoes and a sunhat. It's a good idea to take something to sit on as well, in case the ground is damp or prickly.

Please don't forget to take away your rubbish. I would even go so far as to suggest that you take away rubbish left by other people. Ibiza and Formentera are quite clean islands; do all you can to keep them that way!

16

☀ Country code

The experienced rambler is accustomed to following a 'country code' on his walks, but the tourist out for a lark can unwittingly cause damage, harm animals and even endanger his own life. Please behave responsibly.

- **Do not light fires.** Don't smoke in the pine woods.
- **Leave all gates as you find them** — whether closed or open. The gates do serve a purpose; generally they keep sheep or goats in — or out of — an area.
- **Do not pick wild or cultivated plants.** Some wild flowers are protected by law.
- **Never walk over cultivated land**.
- **Do not walk or cycle on any roads or tracks with 'privado' signs.**
- **Take all your litter away with you**.
- **Walk only on tracks and footpaths.** Crossing rough terrain might be dangerous, or you might not have right of way.
- **Do not walk alone**, and *always* tell someone *exactly* where you are going and what time you plan to return. Remember, if you were to injure yourself, it might be a long time before you were found. On any but a very short walk, take a whistle, torch, some warm clothing and extra rations and water. Don't forget your mobile: the emergency number is **112**. Your mobile will also come in handy if you miss a vital transport connection at the end of a walk or your bicycle breaks down.

Both islands are rich in colourful cultivation; these are pepper plants.

IBIZA

*car tours • walks and
cycle tours • picnics*

❋ Getting about

There's a very good bus service on Ibiza in summer (1 May to 31 October), catering for both the local population and the needs of the tourist. Although there are four different bus companies, they work together and publish one timetable which you can get in the tourist offices and central bus stations in Eivissa, Sant Antoni and Santa Eulària. Timetables change twice in a year: the summer timetable begins on May 1st, the winter timetable on November 1st. Be sure to pick up a new timetable when you arrive on the island or, better still, log on to www.ibizabus.com and check the time-tables in this book just before you travel.

The buses don't have any numbers — you find the destinations on the windscreens. Tickets are inexpensive and can be purchased from the drivers or at kiosks in Eivissa, Sant Antoni and Santa Eulària.

Summer bus and boat timetables are given on pages 131-134; *in winter service is much more limited*. Our printed timetables are for 'work days' only (Mondays to Fridays). On weekends and holidays there are far fewer buses, and these are often very crowded, since many of the local people go visiting then. Avoid the buses on weekends and holidays — make these rest days, or else rent a car — or a bicycle (cycling has become very popular on Ibiza in the last few years; see page 15).

Opposite are plans of Sant Antoni and Santa Eulària; the plan of Eivissa follows on pages 30-31. Bus stops are shown on both plans, which include other helpful tourist information.

Sant Antoni
 1 Tourist information *i*
 2 Post office
 3 Sant Antoni church
 4 Police
 5 Town hall
 6 Lighthouse
 7 Sports ground
 8 Bus station
 9 Club Nautic
10 Market
11 Hospital
🚗 Taxi rank
⛽ Petrol station

Santa Eulària
 1 Tourist information *i*
 2 Bus station
 3 Church
 4 Town hall
 5 Market
 6 Ethnological museum
 7 Roman bridge and old
    Roman road
 8 Hospital
 9 Post office
🚗 Taxi rank
⛽ Petrol station

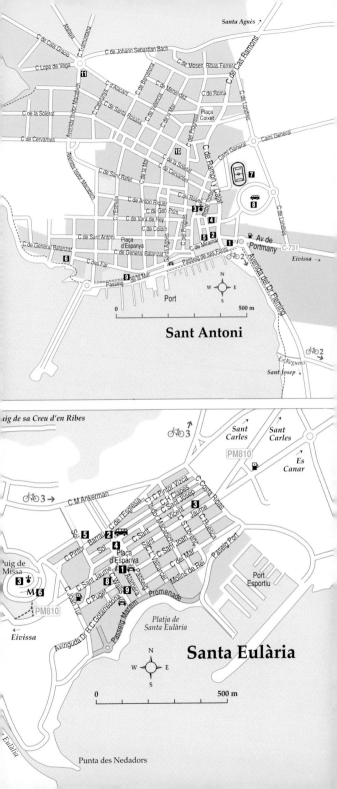

Sant Antoni

- C de Cala Gració
- Tramuntana
- Anabria
- C de Johann Sebastian Bach
- C de Mosén Ribas Ferrer
- C de Cas Ramons
- C Lopa de Vega
- **11**
- C de Barcelona
- C de Menéndez
- C d'Alacant
- C de Roma
- C de Santa Rosalía
- C de la Mar
- C de Valencia
- Plaça Coixet
- Avinguda Isidor Macabich
- C de la Soletat
- C de Progrés
- C de Cervantes
- C de la Soletat
- C de Ramon y Cajal
- Camí General
- Camí General
- Avinguda Isidor Macabich
- C de Sant Rafel
- C de Cervantes
- **10**
- **7**
- C Estella
- C de Anton Riquel
- C de Gebi
- C de Vara de Rey
- Prim
- **3**
- **4**
- C de Colom
- C de Sant Antoni
- Plaça d'Espanya
- Santa Agnès
- C de Rosell
- C del Progrés
- **5**
- **2**
- C de Miramar
- **1**
- Av de Portmany
- C de General Balanzat
- C de General Balanzat
- C de Sant Antoni
- **6**
- C des Far
- Passeig de ses Fonts
- **2**
- C de Londres
- C-731
- Eivissa →
- Avinguda del Dr Fleming
- **9**
- Passeig de la Mar
- Port
- Santa Agnès ↗
- Santa Agnès ↗
- Est Reguetó
- Sant Josep
- **2**

0 — 500 m

N / W · E / S

Santa Eulària

- uig de sa Creu d'en Ribes
- **3**
- Sant Carles
- Sant Carles
- Es Canar
- PM810
- **3**
- C M Ankerman
- C Pintor Vizca
- C l'Església
- C l'Clapes
- Costa Ribas
- **5**
- **2**
- C de l'Església
- C Sant Josep
- C Isidor Macabich
- C Sant Vicent
- C Jaume
- **3**
- C Pintor Barrau
- Sol
- **4**
- C Sant
- C l'Huesca
- Puig de Missa
- Plaça d'Espanya
- C Sant Joan
- Passeig Port
- **3**
- M
- **6**
- C Sant Jaume
- **8**
- **1**
- Alzina
- C del Mar
- Molins de Rey
- Port Esportiu
- C Joan Tur
- C Puget
- **9**
- Promenade
- PM810
- C Calaredona
- Passeig Marítim
- Platja de Santa Eulària
- ← Eivissa
- Avinguda Dr R C Calaredona
- Santa Eulària

0 — 500 m

N / W · E / S

- ↙ Eulalia
- Punta des Nedadors

1 Tourist office *i*
2 Cathedral
3 Episcopal palace
4 Santa Tecla Bastion
5 Archaeological museum
6 Town hall
7 Meat and fish market
8 Gate of the Tablets
9 Castle
10 Portal Nou Bastion
11 Sant Joan Bastion
12 Fruit and vegetable market
13 Casino
14 Clinic
15 Santa Llúcia Bastion
16 Sant Jaume Bastion
17 Sant Bernat Bastion
18 Sant Jordi Bastion
19 Residencia Militar
20 Bullring and museum
21 Post office
22 Bus station
23 Port Authority
24 Museum of Contemporary Art
25 General market
26 Sports ground
27 Puig des Molins Archaeological Museum
28 Punic necropolis
🚕 Taxi rank
⛽ Petrol station

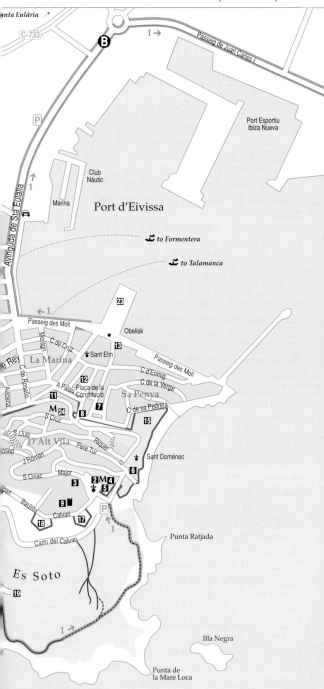

Car tour 1: THE HILLY WEST

Eivissa • Ses Figueretes • Sant Josep • Sant Agusti • Sant Antoni • Sant Rafel • Eivissa

95km/59mi (including the detour routes described); Exit A from Eivissa (see the town plan on pages 22-23)

On route: Picnics (see pages 111-113) 3a-7, 11, 12; Walks 3-7, 11, 12

The tour follows asphalt roads all the way.

Leave **Eivissa** along the Avinguda Macabich (Exit A), heading west past the apartments and holiday bungalows of **Ses Figueretes** (1km ▲▲▲✕☞). You come to the turn-off for the airport and Ses Salines. For a first diversion off the main route, fork left towards Ses Salines on the PM802. Past Platja d'en Bossa (1km left; ▲▲▲✕; Picnics 3a, 3b) you travel through a flat landscape of market gardens and grazing land. Ignore the turn-off to the airport at the little village of **Sant Jordi de ses Salines** (4km ♦) with its attractive church. After 9 km you come to **Sa Canal**, at the salt-pans. Parts of these *salinas* are still in use; centuries ago, the Carthaginians, the Romans and the Arabs took salt from the sea here. The island's most beautiful beach, Platja de Migjorn (also called 'Playa Salinas'; Picnics 3c, 3d), stretches out towards the southeast beyond the pans. Walk 5 ends here; Walk 3 ends just to the north, and Walk 4 passes through as it nears its end.

Head back towards Eivissa now and, back in Sant Jordi, turn off towards the airport. Pass the airport and continue to a stony beach, **Es Codolar** (19km), lying just under the flight path. Walk 5 crosses this beach. A short way further west is the old fishing port of **Sa Caleta** (20km), where you'll find a sandy cove below steep red-sand cliffs. Continue from here to **Cala Jondal** (21km), where there's a white sand beach and a couple of little restaurant beautifully set between old cedars; Walk 5 begins here.

Now head north back to the PM803, leaving the market gardens for pine woods. Stop off at **Cova Santa**★ to see the largest display of stalactites on the island. From here continue on the main road up to **Sant Josep**★ (31km ♦✕☞). Sa Talaiassa, at 487m/1600ft the highest mountain on the island (and setting for Walk 7 and Picnic 7), rises just southwest of Sant Josep.

From Sant Josep head southwest towards Es Cubells. The road winds through a delightful area of olive trees, vineyards and a few grazing fields. Before

24

you get to Es Cubells, fork off left to the little development of **Vista Alegre** (38km 📷), with a fine vantage point down over the sea. When you come to the beautifully-sited settlement of **Es Cubells** (42km ♣✕📷), you'll enjoy fine views over to Formentera. The old monastery here is now a school for priests.

The coves of Sa Caleta and Cala Jondal (Walk 5) lie at the foot of the impressive Fita des Jondal.

View across the Bay of Sant Antoni, with Puig Nunó in the background

From Es Cubells take the high-level 'panorama road' (🎦) southwest to **Cap Llentrisca** (45km).

Return to Es Cubells (48km) and head back towards Sant Josep for a short distance, then turn left towards Cala d'Hort. To park for Walk 6 or Picnic 6, turn off left for 'Torre des Savinar' about 4.5km along. At **Cala d'Hort** (54km 🎦), you enjoy the fine view to Es Vedrà shown on pages 50-51. Return the same way, but take the left turn to **Cala Vedella** (59km ✕). Continue on the winding coast road via **Cala Molí** (65km) to **Cala Tarida** (68km), where Walk 7 ends. From here head through a wood, back to the PM803. Turn right and then left up into **Sant Agusti** (75km ♱), where the church and the nearby Bar Berri are worth a visit.

Return to the PM803 and turn right. You enter lively **Sant Antoni de Portmany★** from the south (80km ♱ ▲▲ ▲ △ ✕ ⊕ ⊕). Walks and Picnics 11 and 12, as well as Cycle tour 2, are reached from here but, apart from the church, there is nothing of interest for the tourist.

From here continue back to Eivissa on the C731. This fast road crosses a pleasant landscape of olive and almond plantations on its arrow-straight 15km-long run back to town. In **Sant Rafel** (88km ♱🎦✕) you might like to take a break to enjoy the views southeast to Ibiza's bay — best appreciated from the church. You're back in **Eivissa** after 95km.

Car tour 2: EAST COAST BEACHES

Eivissa • Roca Llisa • Cala Llonga • Santa Eulària • Cala Pada • Es Canar • Sant Carles • Cala de Sant Vicent • Sant Joan • Sant Llorenç • Eivissa

80km/50mi (including the detour routes described); Exit C from Eivissa (see town plan on pages 22-23).

On route: Picnics (see pages 111-113) 2d, 14, 16-18; Walks 2, 8, 14-23. (Picnic 23 can be reached as a detour from Sant Carles.)

The tour follows asphalt roads throughout. Go slowly and carefully along the steep coastal road from Sant Carles to Cala de Sant Vicent.

Leave **Eivissa** on the C731. At the large roundabout near the town limits, turn right (east) on the C733. Two kilometres along, turn right again, following signposting to **Jesús** (4km ✝). Be sure to visit the 15th-century church here. Then cross an agricultural plain bordered in the southeast by the Serra de Ballansat.

From the plain you climb to the **Coll de Sa Vila** (📷). There is a beautiful view down over the fjord-like bay of Cala Llonga from this pass. Descend past the **Roca Llisa** golf club (10km; Cycle tour 1) into the valley of the Canal de sa Gravada. From the resort of **Cala Llonga★** (13km ▲▲▲✕; Walks 14, 15; Picnic Cycle tour 1), you can make a detour to the lovely sandy beach. Then return to the main road and head gently downhill towards Santa Eulària, skirting the Puig d'en Purredó.

Pine woods interspersed with cultivated fields accompany you to **Santa Eulària des Ríu★** (18km ⓘ✝📷▲▲✕🚌⊕; Walks and Picnics 14, 16-18; Cycle tour 3). The old town and church on the Puig de Missa,

Centuries ago, the local populace sought protection from pirates in defence towers like this one at Balàfia. You will see many of these towers on your tours and walks around the island.

and the Roman bridge, are high points of any visit. To do them justice, you should spend some time here and take the short walk described on page 88 (Walk 18) — but the car tour gives you a delightful first impression of these ancient monuments.

Even if you plan to do the coastal walks in this area, it's worth continuing to Sant Carles via the lovely bays of **Cala Pada** (✕; Walk 17) and **Es Canar** (▲✕; Walks 17 and 19; Cycle tours 4 and 5). This short detour from the more direct route takes you down through pine woods and past market gardens where corn, vegetables, olive and carob trees abound.

Head northwest from Es Canar towards Sant Carles, through wooded hillsides. You pass the old lead mines shown below (on the right). The little village of **Sant Carles de Paralta★** (27km ✝✕; Walks 19-22) is totally unspoilt. Be sure to visit the lovely church shown on page 98. Anita's lively little bar/restaurant, once the meeting place for international drop-outs, now attracts both visitors and foreign residents living locally.

From Sant Carles head down to the beach at **Es Figueral** (31km ✕). The fertile red earth along this stretch supports intensive cultivation of a variety of market-garden produce. Beneath the cliffs you come upon many lovely little sandy bays — and the photogenic column of rock shown opposite.

From Es Figueral take the coastal road towards Cala de Sant Vicent, first passing through plantations of carob and olive trees. Then, after a run through pines, high above the coast, wind down to the bay at **Cala de Sant Vicent★** (35km ✝▲✕; Walk 21). Far too many hotels have been built in this once-lovely little

Anita's bar in Sant Carles: Walk 20 begins on the track to the right.

Santa Eulària and the Puig de Missa; right: Es Paller d'es Camp, a rock column off Es Figueral

bay, but be sure to drive up the steep road to **Punta Grossa** (172m/565ft 📷) for the fabulous views.

Heading west out of Cala de Sant Vicent, you're surrounded by a myriad of oleander bushes in the valley of the Torrent de sa Cala. Here and there terracing interrupts the pine woods. In **Sant Vicent** (45km ✚) turn right through pines down to **Ses Caletes**, a sheltered cove with a small beach and boathouses.

The PM811 winds up to **Sant Joan de Labritja★** (57km ✚✗), a little village set some 200m/650ft above sea level. Be sure to stop at the lovely 18th-century church, where Walk 8 begins. Not far beyond Sant Joan, the PM811 meets the PM733, where you head left (south) through the wide and fertile valley of the Pout d'en Covetes. Just beyond the old defence tower at **Balàfia** (shown on page 27), turn right to **Sant Llorenç** (64km ✚✗); its church has a lovely bell-tower.

Continue south on the PM733. Figs and carobs now take over the landscape. The odd hibiscus brightens the route, as well as the slender stalks of the American aloe. The terrain flattens out. Lovely old *fincas* appear to the left and right, their surrounds graced by fig trees under which sheep graze. And in between the farms, the rich red soil of Ibiza positively *glows*. All too soon the factories and oil tanks come into view. At the roundabout turn left, back into **Eivissa** (80km).

Car tour 3: RURAL IBIZA

Eivissa • Santa Gertrudis • Portinatx • Cala d'en Serra • Port de Sant Miquel • Sant Miquel • Isla Blanca • Sant Mateu • Santa Agnès • Sant Rafel • Eivissa

106km/66mi (including the detour routes described); Exit C from Eivissa (see the town plan on pages 22-23)

On route: Picnic (see pages 111-113) 9a, 9b, 10, 13; Walks 9, 10, 13

While all the roads along this tour are asphalted, they are sometimes very narrow — so do drive slowly.

Leave **Eivissa** from Exit C, turning right at the roundabout on the north side of the city. Heading northeast on the PM733, you pass through the unattractive suburbs. But soon the industrial ugliness is behind you and you're rolling through lemon groves and plantations of carobs, olives and figs. You'll even spot the odd patch of apricots growing along this stretch. At first the terrain is flat, and the high hills lie some way off. The owners of the little *fincas* along the road all keep sheep and goats. Soon light scatterings of pine trees punctuate the breaks between farms.

Some 5.5km along, by the Ca'n Clavos estate, fork left towards Santa Gertrudis and Sant Miquel on the PM804. The little village of **Santa Gertrudis** (11km ♣✕) lies just about in the centre of the island; it attracts artists and writers. The pretty white church is topped by a bell-tower. Head northeast from Santa Gertrudis via **Sant Llorenç**, then follow the main C733 to where it ends in **Portinatx★** (37km ▲▲♠✕). Walk 8 ends here; Walk 9 and Picnic 9a begin here.

On your return from Portinatx take a little detour to the bay of **Cala d'en Serra** (▨; Walk 8), to enjoy the view down into the deep bay. Then head back to the main road and retrace your route, making short visits to **Cala Xuclà** and **Cala Xarraca** (Picnic 9b), both of them on the route of Walk 9.

Not far beyond the junction with the road from Sant Joan, branch off right towards Sant Miquel. Leave this road 2.5 km along and turn right to **Cala Benniràs**. An old stretch of road takes you down to **Port de Sant Miquel** (✕), from where Walk and Picnic 10 set out.

Continuing south, a detour to the peninsula of **Na Xamena** is called for (61km ▲▲). Head towards Punta de sa Creu as far as the helicopter landing pad. From here a lane takes you south through woods and cultivation, back to the main road.

In **Sant Miquel de la Balensat★** (67 km ♣▨✕),

where the church once served as a refuge for the community during ancient pirate raids, follow signs for Portitxol. You will reach the settlement of **Isla Blanca** (73km 🖼) with fabulous views over the north coast. From here head south, cross back over the ridge to the Sant Mateu road, and turn right. The little village of **Sant Mateu d'Aubarca** (84km ♆✕) has picturesque church atop a hill in an enchanting landscape.

Continue on a narrow asphalt road following signposting to the widely-scattered village of **Santa Agnès de Corona** (88km ♆✕), with a small restaurant beside the church. Walk 13 begins and ends here; its short version leads to Picnic 13. From Santa Agnès head

south through woods and fields to **Sant Rafel** (99km ♆🖼✕), where you pick up the PM731 dual carriageway back to **Eivissa** (106km).

Church at Sant Mateu (top) and Cala Benniràs (below)

Walk 1: D'ALT VILA • ES SOTO • ES BOTAFOC • TALAMANCA

See plan on pages 22-23 to begin, then map on pages 36-37.

Distance: about 9km/5.5mi; 3h

Grade: easy — with a bit of climbing around D'Alt Vila

Equipment: stout shoes, long trousers for the coastal walk across Es Soto, swimwear; see also page 10 (top)

How to get there: The walk begins in Eivissa.
To return: 🚢 or 🚌 from Talamanca

A short stroll to D'Alt Vila (the ancient centre), the coastal area called Es Soto and the Botafoc light-house on the peninsula of Sa Mola is a lovely way to spend half a day near the capital. Time is immaterial and will depend on how many places you stop to visit.

Start the walk at the **Passeig de Vara de Rey** (by 1 on the plan) and climb up through the narrow streets to the beautiful old town. No specific route is shown for this part of the walk; explore at leisure. After enjoying the views over the sea from the **Baluard de Sant Bernat** (17), continue round the battlements to the tunnel under the Portal Nou Bastion on the western side of D'Alt Vila (**1h**).

Walk down the steps to Carrer de Joan Xico and follow it uphill to the left. At a junction, go left on Carrer de Ramón Muntaner, through a tunnel, and take the next fork to the left. This road leads to the **Residencia Militar** (19). In front of the iron gate, follow the track to the right, down to the seaside. You look out to three small rocky islands (Illa Negra, Sa Corbeta and Illa de ses Rates), with Formentera in the far distance. Follow the wide track in a bend to the left and, when it ends, continue on a stony path climbing over the rocky ground of **Es Soto** (Picnic 1a). This area would make an excellent recreation area, so close to town. Soon you have a

Lighthouse in Eivissa harbour

view of the harbour. As the path turns towards the castle, you'll see some old ruins; they may date from Punic times. At a fork, head right downhill. The path, in places slightly overgrown, narrows and eventually joins another path leading to the castle. Follow this across the coastal rocks (there are some old red waymarks), soon heading towards the cathedral and nearby car park. On the last stretch, before the city wall, the path is again slightly overgrown. When you reach the car park, turn right and walk down the steps, and take the footpath through the tunnel, back into D'Alt Vila (**2h**). (If you turn left, you come to another tunnel which leads straight to the cathedral.)

Leaving D'Alt Vila, continue by walking along the promenade, passing the place where the boats to Formentera tie up and a sun dial in the shape of a drum. The promenade ends at the fenced-in marina. You can get into the marina at the **Club Naútic** — a worthwhile detour, if you want to take some appealing photographs — but you have to leave the same way.

From the marina follow the little-used road; fences either side separate it from both the main road and the yachts. In a few minutes you can get back down to the quay. A bronze monument is passed at the container port, but this area is off-bounds for walkers.

Then continue southeast along the palm-lined

Es Soto (Picnic 1a), with the Residencia Militar at the left

promenade, passing the Edificio Marítimo and an old anchor in front of the Comandancia de Marina. Now follow the newer promenade which begins here. You cross a channelled streambed at the Jackpot Casino. Shortly after, the road takes you past the pretty Dino V restaurant. Four minutes later, when the Club El Divino (with a fountain in front) is on your right, you can either continue along the promenade or follow the green-painted concrete walkway by the quay. When you reach the **Botafoc Marina**, you can see the Hotel El Corso (where Walks 2 begins) behind it. From the roundabout before the El Corso, follow the new promenade south to **Botafoc lighthouse** (Picnic 1b).

From the lighthouse make your way over to the Illa Grossa peninsula. There are short-cut steps to the peninsula, but the gate in front of them is usually locked. If so, retrace your outgoing route to a rough track heading southeast. Follow this as it curls up to the **highest point on Illa Grossa**, where there are some old foundations dating from World War II (Picnic 1c). In the northeast the cliffs drop straight down to the sea — take care, the cliff-edge is unprotected.

Returning from the Illa Grossa, make your way back to Illa Plana along the seaside road, passing hotels and villas. You reach the beach at **Talamanca** by the **Bar Flotante** (**2h30min**). Walk the whole length of this beautiful beach (Picnic 2a) — either on the boardwalk or the shore. Then retrace your steps to **Talamanca's little pier** where the boat to Eivissa moors (**3h**). In winter, when the boats don't run, head to the **bus stop** at the roundabout by the Hotel El Corso.

Walk 2: TALAMANCA • PUIG D'EN MANYA • TALAMANCA

Distance: 9km/5.6mi; 3h

Grade: easy, with overall ascents/descents of about 150m, but you must be sure-footed for the descent to the rocks at Cap Martinet.

Equipment: lightweight walking boots (you need good ankle support), swimwear, picnic, water; see also page 10 (top)

How to get there and return: ⛴ or 🚌 from Eivissa to Talamanca and return (the ferry is more fun, but only runs in summer).

Short walk: Follow the walk as far as you like; return the same way.

You can enjoy this coastal walk at any time of year; although it's quite short, allow a full day. The walk used to run all the way to Cala Llonga, but a landslide has destroyed the beautiful path in the Torres Baixes area, where a villa on the 142m-high hill prevents you going round the damaged area. Eventually the path will probably be repaired — although it will be a big job!

Start the walk at the **Botafoc roundabout**. There is a bus stop, and it's not far from the ferry landing. Head north to the seaside that starts at the **Bar Flotante** (a good place to take a break at the end of the walk). Walk along the beach, **Cala Talamanca** for 10 minutes (Picnic 2a) — either on the sand or the boardwalk. In the morning you may have the beach all to yourself.

When the boardwalk ends, continue along the promenade. Pass a few hotels and, when the promenade ends, carry on beside the sea, initially on a good coastal track. Always keep beside the sea, ignoring all routes inland. You pass some boathouses and two restaurants. Soon the path leads uphill; you cross the **Punta de s'Andreus** and later walk to the seaward side of the Club Paradise holiday apartments. To the right there is a beautiful view over to Formentera.

Before long the route is blocked by a high metal

Coastal rocks at Cap Martinet (Picnic 2b)

fence surrounding a large building. 'Electrica Pittiusas' is written on the western side of the building. Turn left inland here, and you'll see that the northern side of the building bears the inscription 'Asociación Insular de Tiro Olímpico' (clay pigeon shooters' association). This former military building is obviously now used for

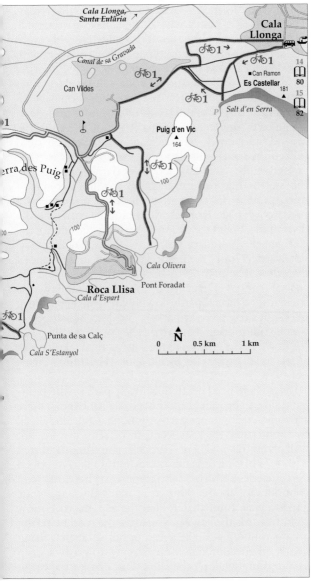

different purposes. Pass this building and a small sports field, then turn right and right again, along a lane running back to the sea. Now on the far side of the multi-purpose building, you can pick up the narrow path again, heading eastwards.

Soon you can make a short dog-leg to see some

wonderfully-formed coastal rocks at **Cap Martinet**. There are two places where you'll have to scramble down stone 'steps' (they are at the cliff edge at the right of the point itself). Not everyone will be confident with this descent — *and it is not recommended when the wind is blowing!* — but the sure of foot will be able to get down easily to the impressive rocks shown on page 35 (**1h**; Picnic 2b). You can see into three *calas* from here. You'll cross the first one (Cala Roja) on the cliffs, the second (un-named) via a wall, and just behind the third (also un-named) is the landslide area.

Return the same way and, after clambering back up the 'steps', head towards a cluster of villas a couple of minutes away. Shortly after, the path goes round a pretty cove, **Cala Roja**. At this point the path is hardly discernible, but make your way between the edge of the cliff and the boundary wall of the villas, heading east-northeast. (Notice the mock defence tower near one of the villas. The path leads between the tower and the coastal rocks.) Don't turn inland, but follow the strongest of several paths downhill to a small bay (you may spot a few red waymarks). The descent is steep, so watch your footing. Cross the valley on a retaining wall (or down in the bottom of the valley), then take a break at the cove, a pleasant picnic spot (**1h10min**; Picnic 2c).

From here head north up a lovely path on the right-hand side of the valley (another good picnic spot); there are some shallow steps part-way along. Continue ahead to a motorable track; it seems to be semi-private, but walkers are allowed here. Turn left: you come to an arch with two black iron gates on the left. One is inscribed 'Sa Canal de sa Murta'. Turn right (east) here; the road continues for about 100m/yds, passing through a wide gap in a wall. Immediately after the gap, the road turns right towards the sea, but you leave the road by taking a path running straight ahead uphill — at first rising gently, then climbing more steeply towards a deep fissure running along the cliffs. You can see the cairn-marked path running ahead alongside stone walls, with the landslide area beside it. Below is a deep, un-named *cala*. This is where the walk ends (**2h**), near **Puig d'en Manya** — until the path is rebuilt (*do* let me know, in care of Sunflower, if it is!). A fence prohibits you climbing any further. Retrace your outgoing route to the **Botafoc roundabout** (**3h**).

Cycle tour 1: EIVISSA • CALA LLONGA • SALT D'EN SERRA • EIVISSA

See the map on pages 36-37, as well as the touring map

Distance: 45km/28mi; 5h

Grade: fairly strenuous, with overall ascents of about 400m/1300ft

Equipment: swimwear, picnic, water; see also page 10 (top)

Short tour: Follow the main tour, but omit some of the *calas*.

Start this tour very early in the morning, to avoid the rush hour traffic in the capital — and return at *siesta* time in the afternoon. That way you will meet as little traffic as possible. This tour crosses a landscape of gardens, runs past the island's golf course, and dips into one cove after another. Plan a long break at the easternmost point of the tour — either having a swim

This cycle tour shows you rural Ibiza at its best, even though some of the once-proud fincas *are falling into ruins.*

and restaurant meal at Cala Llonga or a swim and picnic at the quiet cove of Salt d'en Serra.

Start out along the **promenade in Eivissa** (as Walk 1), and cycle along to the **Botafoc roundabout**. Turn left there and take the next right, to the Bar Flotante at the start of **Cala Talamanca**. Head north past the bar to a crossroads and go straight over. Now you leave the asphalt and head north-northwest on a pretty track with virtually no traffic, **Ses Feixes**, with impressive garden entrances (*feixes*). The track soon joins the asphalt road again in front of a hotel near the eastern end of Cala Talamanca. Turn left here; in a minute you're at the **Talamanca roundabout**, where you turn left again.

Now you can use the pavement as you cycle northwest, then north, towards Jesús. After just over 500m, watch for a brown arrow signpost, and turn right on the asphalt road signposted to Cala Estanyol, heading east-northeast Remain on this road for about 1.5km, then take the track to the right; a multicoloured stone here indicates the way to Cala Estanyol. Ride east downhill along the deep valley of the *torrent* on your left. Roca Llisa is very close by now, but can only be reached from here on foot. Have a swim and a picnic at beautiful **Cala S'Estanyol** (about 9km).

The cycle back up past the junction with the multicoloured stone and back to the road to Jesús. Continue north to **Jesús**. Visit the famous little church (on the corner where you will turn right uphill to continue the tour). There's an old waterwheel well in the churchyard.

Now continue northeast uphill for 3km, to the **Col**

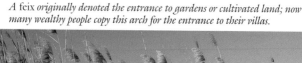

A feix originally denoted the entrance to gardens or cultivated land; now many wealthy people copy this arch for the entrance to their villas.

Reconstruction of an old well with waterwheel by the church at Jesús; the waterwheel was originally driven by men or animals.

de Sa Vila (at the KM4 road marker). From here it's all downhill to the domain of the seriously rich — **Roca Llisa**, south of the golf course. It's interesting to look around and ponder: would I like to live in this atmosphere? Some villas are arranged in crescent style — called an *anfiteatro*.

Return steeply uphill and turn right before the golf course, following signposting to Cala Olivera. After about 400m turn right down a track to **Cala Olivera**, a nice little bay where you can swim.

Return once more to the asphalt road. Head right (north) for about 400m, then, south of the golf course, turn right (east) on another track (marked with green waymark posts). Keep left at the end of the golf course, and turn sharp left after about 150m. The track first takes you a short way west, but turn right at the villa El Palmero, heading east downhill to **Cala Llonga** (30km). Have a long break here for a swim and a good meal — unless you are going to picnic at Salt d'en Serra.

The last beach on the tour is **Salt d'en Serra** (Picnic CT1), only 1.5km away by track (first head west, then south). From the Salt d'en Serra restaurant head northwest, to the track south of the golf course. Now, with most of the hard work behind you (save for the pull up to the Col de Vila), retrace your route back to Jesús and Talamanca. After turning right at the Talamanca roundabout, you can either turn right again along Ses Feixes, or turn left further on, directly back to the Bar Flotante. From there take your outgoing route back to **Eivissa** (45km; **5h**).

Walk 3: FROM PLATJA D'EN BOSSA TO PLATJA DE MIGJORN

See photographs on pages 46, 47, 111

Distance: 10km/6.2mi; 3h20min

Grade: easy; overall ascents/descents of about 300m/1000ft

Equipment: lightweight walking boots, water, picnic, swimwear; see also page 10 (top)

How to get there: 🚌 from Eivissa to Platja d'en Bossa

To return: 🚌 from Sa Canal to Eivissa (only in summer; in winter pre-arranged taxi from the PM802 at the Platja de Migjorn)

Short walk: Follow the main walk for as long as you like and return the same way.

You can enjoy this coastal walk any time of year. In winter it will take only a morning or afternoon, but in summer allow a full day — even then the sea breeze should prevent you feeling uncomfortably hot. The walk is marked throughout by red dots and blue triangles or blue arrows indicating a change of direction.

Begin the walk at **Platja d'en Bossa** by going south past the hotels and tennis courts. Some salt-pans will be on your right, with the airport behind them. A watchtower punctuates the end of the beach ahead. Four minutes along you cross a salt-water canal on a wooden bridge. Continue beside the **canal**, which is hemmed in by high stone walls. Then follow the coastal path uphill to the **Torre de sa Sal Rossa** (**10-15min**; Picnic 3a).

From here descend to some boathouses and make for the coast. You soon pass a second lot of boathouses. Several paths branch off to the right uphill here. Keep to the higher path; the path just a few metres above the sea soon becomes almost indiscernible. Soon the path begins to climb and, as you gain height, you may spot a few fishermen on the coast. Enjoy the solitude of this coastal landscape, with rocks on your left and the first trees of a pine wood appearing on the right. Underfoot, the rocks are sharp and spiky.

The path leads away from the sea, to keep clear of the cliff-edge and its dangerous, sheer drops. When you reach high ground, you look down into a cove and see the path that will take you up and over the other side. As you approach the **cove** (**40min**), however, you'll find that the rocky shoreline is too steep for you to get down for a swim. Climb out of the inlet on the excellent path, soon coming close to the coast again. You pass a small circular stone fireplace. The coastal rocks are razor-sharp, the terrain still hostile to swimmers. Three minutes from the cove you cross the next crest, some

42

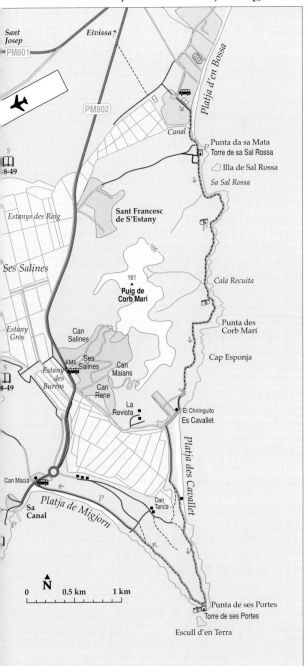

100m/yds inland. But soon you're back near the sea again, and the path runs through a **little pine wood** (**50min**; Picnic 3b) — a lovely spot, similar to the setting shown opposite.

From here the path runs inland, crosses a crest and then descends into another hollow, where you may find rubbish strewn about. A few minutes later the path again climbs away from the sea, and from the next crest, above the **Punta d'es Corb Marí**, you can see all the way to another watchtower, the Torre de ses Portes; it marks the southernmost tip of Ibiza. Now head steeply downhill; when you come to the next inlet, you can finally take a swim.

From here the way climbs gently through dwarf pines, then skirts the cliff-edge before bending back inland and running steeply downhill. Now another steep climb and descent await you. When you come to a fork (about eight minutes after heading inland) take the upper path. This takes you to a **concrete lane**. Follow this to the left downhill, but then fork left after about 20 metres/yards. You come to some holiday homes, the **restaurant El Chiringuito** and then a small **bar** at the start of **Es Cavallet** beach (**2h**; one of the few official naturist beaches on the island and frequented by gays).

Now you *could* just make straight for the watchtower by crossing the beach. But I prefer the pretty route behind the dunes: pick up the good track which heads south from the inland side of the large parking area and follow it between the salt-pans and the pine-fringed sand dunes. Just before the end of the salt-pans fork left in the pine wood, again following a sandy track. Keep left at another fork, to reach the sea by another small **bar**. The hard-packed sand at the water's edge makes for easier walking. Five minutes along, the beach ends; continue along the good coastal path above the stony cliffs to the **Torre de ses Portes** (**2h30min**).

Take a break in its shade, look back the way you've come, and then follow the ongoing path through a bizarre coastal landscape. Sandy little coves glisten between the sharp dark rocks. Eventually you reach the bars and restaurants at **Platja de Migjorn** ('Playa Salinas'; **3h05min**; Picnic 3c). The beach ends at the old salt-loading place at **Sa Canal** (Picnic 3d); the bus stops on the **PM802** to Eivissa (**3h20min**), a short way uphill to the right (by the restaurant Can Macià).

Walk 4: CAP D'ES FALCO

Distance: 13km/8mi; 4h

Grade: easy at first, but after the restaurant Cap d'es Falcó you must be sure-footed and have a head for heights (the path often runs just beside the cliff-edge); overall ascents/descents about 500m/1650ft.

Equipment: lightweight walking boots, water, picnic, swimwear; see also page 10 (top)

How to get there: 'Salinas' 🚌 from Eivissa; alight at the KM4 road marker on the PM802 (tell the bus driver to let you off there).
To return: the same bus, boarding at the Platja de Migjorn (only in summer; in winter pre-arranged taxi from the restaurant Can Macià)

Allow a whole day for this beautiful walk abounding with lovely picnic spots with splendid views. You'll probably have it all to yourself, although the airport and capital are not very far away. *Do note* that stout shoes are very important on this walk, and don't attempt it after rainfall, when the soil may be still wet.

Start the walk at the **KM4 road marker** on the PM802. Take the track into the **Estany des Burros** (one of the salt pans) on your left. Turn left after about 100m/yds, to cross to the far side of these *salinas*. Soon you walk round a hill of pure salt; you could take away a bagful, but it's too early in the walk, so take some if you follow Walk 5, when you pass this salt hill near the end of the walk. Then, at a T-junction with an almost-white, sandy track, turn right. This track, with red metal waymarking posts, now takes you west, with the salt pans on your right and woods on your left.

At **Pont de Baix (1h)** you come upon the excellent restaurant Cap d'es Falcó, with a view to Es Vedrà. Take

Picnic 3d: the coast just west of Sa Canal

a break here before you start the climb. From the restaurant, follow the **green waymarks**, heading south-southeast, climbing above the cliffs. The narrow path leads you up and down over several low peaks — all with an altitude of about 120m/395ft. Once in a while you can see the sea. Walkers who suffer from vertigo should keep away from the edge of the cliffs. When you have descended from the last peak (126m) above the **Cap d'es Falcó (2h)**, the path turns left into the valley of **Canal de s'Olla**. You now walk southeast and soon pick up **blue waymarks**. The path is a bit overgrown

View north over the salt pans and the stony Codolar coast, with the restaurant Cap d'es Falcó in the foreground; opposite: the salt factory

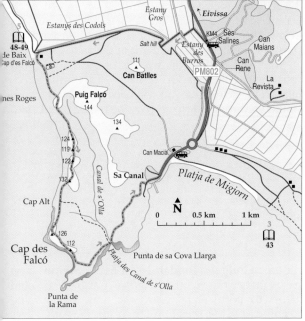

in places, but you can't get lost: follow the blue waymarks. Have a rest and a swim at the tiny beach, **Platja des Canal de s'Olla** (**3h**).

From here the path climbs back to about 80m before you descend to **Sa Canal** and the salt works — still producing salt. Follow the road past the buildings, to the bar/restaurant **Can Macià** (**4h**), where you can catch a bus back to Eivissa — or meet your pre-arranged taxi, if you're walking in winter.

Walk 5: FROM CALA JONDAL TO SA CANAL

See photographs on pages 25, 45, 46, 47, 111

Distance: 12km/7.4mi; 4h

Grade: easy, with one ascent/descent of about 160m/520ft, but you must be sure-footed and have a head for heights on Puig des Jondal. During the bird-breeding season the route over the salt pans is closed, and you will have to use the path along Es Codolar

Equipment: lightweight walking boots, long trousers, water, picnic, swimwear; see also page 10 (top)

How to get there: Cala Vedella 🚌 to the stop above Cala Jondal; otherwise 🚕 taxi to the restaurants at Cala Jondal (cheaper if you first take a bus to the airport and taxi from there).

To return: 🚌 from Sa Canal to Eivissa (only in summer; in winter pre-arranged taxi from the bar/restaurant Can Macià on the PM802)

M ake a day of this super walk. There are several lovely picnic spots — on Puig des Jondal, at Sa Caleta or Es Codolar, in the salt pans or in the woods below Puig Falcó. And four restaurants! — two at the start, one in the middle and one at the end.

Start the walk at the sea side of the **Cala Jondal** restaurants (Blue Marlin, Yemanja). Climb the good, but steep (sometimes you will need your hands) path southeast through the woods, along the cliffs and up to

the top of **Puig des Jondal** (157m/515ft; **30min**). You have a marvellous view to the *salinas,* Cap d'es Falcó and across to Formentera. Cross the peak and descend steeply eastwards, then north. In places the path is very mossy, so take special care after rain! About 100m short of some houses, the path runs into a track. Follow this to the left, descending more gently. Soon you come back to your ascent path; take care on the last, steep descent, then have a break at one of the restaurants (**1h**).

Walk back 200m/yds to the asphalt road and turn right. After 500m ignore a track off right to 'Campament de Cala Jondal' (the pretty *finca* opposite was once the 'Casa de Bang Bang', owned by Kate Middleton's uncle Gary). Take the *next* track to the right, and follow it down to the sea. Turn left and, ignoring routes inland, keep by the coast. You pass a small bar below the cliffs, some derelict World War II fortifications, and the fenced site of a Phoenician village dating from the 7th century BC. And you may meet some men practising the 2000 year old sport of flinging stones with a rope. The Spanish name for the Balearic Islands ('Baleares') derives from this sport. Eventually the path passes some boathouses at the small bay of **Sa Caleta** (**2h**).

From here you have to walk along the road for a short time, but leave it before a small supermarket (*'Comestibles'*), to follow a wide track above the stony beach of **Es Codolar** — at first with the airport on your left, and later the salt pans. This area is now a bird sanctuary, and with luck you may see flamingoes.

Take a break at the **restaurant Cap d'es Falcó** (**3h**). Then head east through the *salinas* on a track marked with red metal posts. When you meet the PM802 turn right. Keep right at the Es Cavallet junction, then use the walkway on the east side of the road to a **roundabout**. Continue south for 200m, to the bar/restaurant **Can Macià** (**4h**), to catch a bus or meet your taxi.

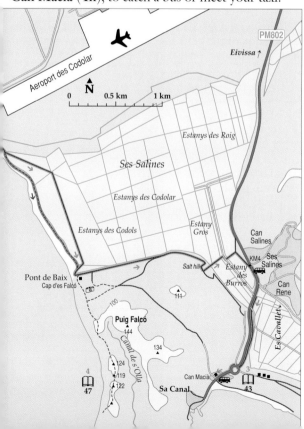

Walk 6: TORRE DES SAVINAR

See also cover photograph   **Distance:** 1.5km/1mi; 1h

Grade: easy, but you must be sure-footed to do the entire circuit; overall ascent/descent of just over 150m/500ft

Equipment: lightweight walking boots, water; see also page 10 (top)

How to get there and return: 🚗 hired car to the Torre des Savinar track. Go via Sant Josep and from there take the Cala d'Hort road. The track you want is *not* signposted; it is some 1.6km short of Cala d'Hort, where the asphalt road makes a near 90° turn to the right. Turn left (asphalted for a few metres), and park 600m along, at a mini-roundabout where the track ahead is blocked off with boulders.

Short walk: Just climb to the tower and return the same way (easy; 40min return; stout shoes will suffice).

O n this short walk you enjoy one of the finest views on Ibiza: from the 241m/800ft-high hill you look out over the Torre des Savinar and towards the fairy-tale rock Es Vedrà — seen on many postcards.

From the **mini-roundabout** where you parked, **start out** by continuing along the track blocked to traffic by boulders. You can see the watchtower (Torre des Savinar) ahead to the left. A minute later Es Vedrà rises in full beauty in front of you. To the right you look towards Cala d'Hort with the little island, Escull de Cala d'Hort, in front of it.

When you reach the **Mirador des Savinar (10min)** at the edge of the cliffs, you'll find many lovely picnic spots under pines or dwarf pines (Picnic 6) — all sharing the fairy-tale view. From here climb the good but stony path up to the 18th-century **Torre des Savinar (20min)**; it is very well preserved.

The short walk turns back here, but those of you who are sure-footed should continue

Whether you enjoy the view from the beach at Cala d'Hort or higher up —and whether on a clear day or in mist — the island of Es Vedrà is the iconic landmark of Ibiza.

round the coast, following traces of a path along the crest. Soon you reach some big rocks. Continue *carefully* in a northeasterly direction to the **highest point of the walk** at 241m/800ft (**30min**). From this high point, shown overleaf,
you look out over the watchtower to Es Vedrà and Es Vedranell.

Those of you unused to difficult mountain paths should retrace your steps from here, as the descent on the far side of the rise is tricky and potentially dangerous. The main walk continues ahead, however: descend very carefully. The path peters out, and you have to make your own way over the chalky rock. Within ten minutes you'll pick up a path again coming from the northwestern side of the hill. It goes over rocks and through scrub, in three minutes bending to the right, towards another viewpoint. You descend over gravel for another couple of minutes — back to the edge

Wonderful view to Es Vedrà rising above mist and the Torre des Savinar

of the cliffs, and another fine **viewpoint** down into the Cala de Sa Pedra d'es Savinar. (The fence can be ignored — it's even broken in some places.)

(*Experts* could make the very steep, skiddy descent of 150m/500ft to this little bay; the various paths all merge further down and the main path runs about 20m to the left of the vertical cliff wall. It takes 20-25 minutes to get down to the plateau, where there was once a sandstone quarry (Sa Pedra d'es Savinar). The cove and quarry became a haunt of the Flower Children in the 1960s, and there are still sculptures of Buddha and the like. More recently, MTV aired a couple of big outdoor parties in the quarry.)

From the cliffs head north, back to the **mini-roundabout** where you parked (**1h**).

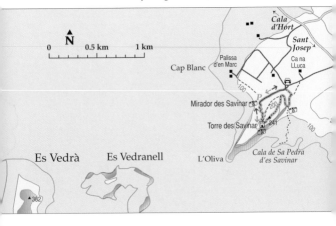

Walk 7: SANT JOSEP • SA TALAIASSA • CALA TARIDA

Distance: 18km/11.2mi; 6h

Grade: fairly strenuous and long, with an ascent of 300m/1000ft and descent of 500m/1640ft

Equipment: lightweight walking boots, long trousers, picnic, water, swimwear; see also page 10 (top)

How to get there: 🚌 from Eivissa or Sant Antoni to Sant Josep
To return: 🚌 from Cala Tarida to Eivissa or Sant Antoni

Shorter walk: Sant Josep — Sa Talaiassa — Sant Josep (9km/5.6mi; 3h; moderate, with an ascent/descent of about 280m/920ft; access by 🚌 from Eivissa or Sant Antoni to/from Sant Josep). Follow the main walk, turning right at the junction at the 1h50min-point and descending the motorable track. Some 450m before you reach the asphalt road from Cala Vedella, turn right uphill on a track going off at a 45° angle. (If you pass three driveways on the right in quick succession, you have gone too far.) You quickly pass Can Vicent Jeroni, after which you should see a green post waymarking the route. You then pass Can Font Figuera and meet the Cala Vedella road 1km west of Sant Josep. Follow the road to the right, back to Sant Josep.

Alternative walks

1) Sant Josep — Sa Talaiassa — Sant Josep (14km/8.7mi; 5h; fairly strenuous, with an ascent/descent of a little over 300m/1000ft; access by 🚌 from Eivissa or Sant Antoni to/from Sant Josep). Follow the main walk as far as the T-junction met at the 1h50min-point, where the main walk goes right. Go left (south) here, soon passing an old fig tree. Then, after 300m/yds, turn left (southeast) on another track. It runs parallel with Es Torrentas in the deep valley to your left. Some 500m/yds along, after a bend to the right, fork left downhill. Ignore the sign 'camino cortado'. Ignore a similar sign further downhill and carry straight on past a chain barrier. Keep to the left of a field and pass an attractive *finca*. You join another track used by cycle routes 7 and 12. The cycle routes cross a valley. Don't follow them; instead, keep straight ahead (northeast). The last part of this track is tarred, and then you come to the Sant Josep/Es Cubells road (PM803-1). Follow this road for just 40m/yds, then turn right on a track (surfaced initially). Keep right at a fork almost at once. Just under 1km along, turn sharp left on another track. This soon becomes a lane and bends right to another lane, the Cami des Verger. Follow this due north to rejoin the PM803-1 which takes you back into Sant Josep (5h).

2) Sant Josep — Sa Talaiassa — Roques Altes — Es Vedrà view — Sant Josep (13km/8mi; 4h30min; fairly strenuous, with an ascent/descent of 350m/1150ft; access by 🚌 from Eivissa or Sant Antoni to/from Sant Josep). Follow the main walk to the T-junction at the 1h50min-point and then for a further 300m/yds, to where Alternative walk 1 turns left. Keep right here (southwest). Ignore a turn-off to the left. When the motorable track ends at a parking area, head right (west-northwest) to a memorial to the people killed in a plane crash on the Roques Altes ridge in 1972. En route you pass an old charcoal-burning place *(sitja)*. From the memorial continue a short way further in the same direction — to the edge of the cliff, from where there is a wonderful view along the west coast of the island. Then return to the parking area and follow the cul-de-sac track southwest. In under 20 minutes it takes you to an unsurpassed view over towards Es Vedrà. Return the same way to the parking area and then retrace your steps back to Sa Talaiassa and Sant Josep.

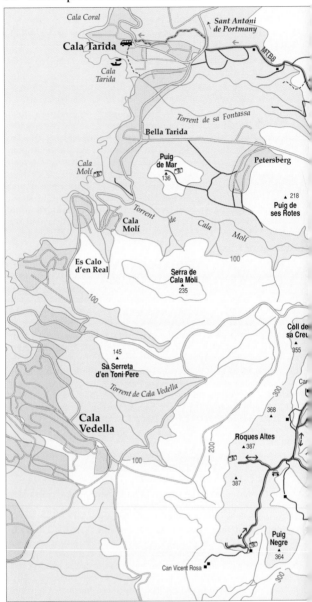

This walk takes you to the highest point on the island and then down to the west coast. On a clear day you'll have wonderful views over the whole of Ibiza from the TV transmitter shortly before the summit of Sa Talaiassa. From here forests and market gardens lead

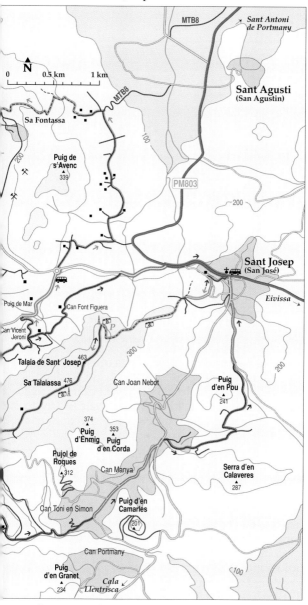

you down to Cala Tarida, where you can end this long but lovely walk with a swim.

From the bus stop in **Sant Josep** walk back to the main road, to where the **walk begins** opposite the **church**. Pick up a signposted cobbled trail waymarked

View northwest on the ascent to Sa Talaiassa, with the island of S'Espartar in the distance

in blue. Turn right at the first fork (after just 20m/yds) and then left uphill (almost at once). When the cobbles give way to gravel, continue to a hotel and then turn left up the tarred lane. After 250m/yds, fork right on another lane and follow this for a good five minutes, until a sign points the way up a steep path. Almost immediately you'll see the two masts of the TV transmitter on the northeast side of the ridge. The aroma of thyme accompanies you and, if you're a photographer, you will find plenty of good subjects as you climb. To your right, for example, are wonderful views across the Badia de Sant Antoni. Steps have been cut into the rock to help you gain height on the steeper sections of the trail. A short descent takes you down to a saddle. Just before the ridge, the trail goes past an old charcoal-burning place *(sitja)*. At the ridge (452m/ 1800ft; **1h**; Picnic 7), both small transmitter masts are in front of you on the right. Take a short break here and enjoy the views — which are in fact better than those from higher up. To the north you overlook the Badia de Sant Antoni, to the south the plains above Es Cubells.

Continue the walk along the motorable access track, heading towards the larger mast. In a few minutes you pass the little relay station. The large mast on **Sa Talaiassa** (476m/1560ft; under **1h15min**) marks the highest point on the island, guarded by some keen dogs.

From here continue along the motorable track, which now descends gently. There are some very attractive picnic spots among the pines along the ridge. About 10 minutes down a track branches off to the right; ignore it — it only goes to a house. Continue along the main track, not far below the crest. Ignore the turn-off to the left after another five minutes, and follow the track in a gentle bend to the right. You'll be overlooking the offshore islands, which are particularly attractive in the morning sun. Later on, the track runs along the other side of the ridge, and you have good views of the pine forest and over Platja de Migjorn on the south coast. Then a canyon-like ravine opens up on your left.

Soon you reach a **major T-junction** (**1h50min**). Go right here *(both Alternative walks go left)*. The track heads straight for the coastal rocks of Cap Nunó north of Punta de sa Galera; they appear to block the northern side of Sant Antoni Bay. To the left of the track are some magnificent fig trees; their large branches offer ideal shade for a picnic. Four-five minutes from the junction, ignore a small track on the left; it only goes to a farm. Continue straight ahead, with both transmitter masts in view in front of you. As you descend, ignore all turn-offs left and right. *(But if you are doing the Short walk, watch out for your track on the right.)*

Eventually you meet an **asphalt road** (**2h30min**). It runs from Sant Josep via the Coll de Sa Creu to Cala Vedella. Follow it to the east (right). The road bends left, to head north through the valley. Four-five minutes along the road you come to a **bus stop** (summer buses to Cala Vedella, Sant Antoni and Sant Josep). Continue north for 100m/yds, to a **roundabout**, where a left goes to Cala Tarida and right to Sant Josep. Ignore these roads; instead take the track on the far side of the

The Talaiassa range at sunset, from the Formentera ferry

Wooden waymarking post on mountain bike route 8.

roundabout, heading northeast. (This track will eventually round the east side of Puig de s'Avenc.) Walking down the track, ignore all turn-offs to the left. You pass a house with the number 4364. To the right is a fertile valley, backed by mountains.

After a fairly steep descent you come to a T-junction. Turn right past lovely gardens and *fincas,* down to another T-junction. This time turn left (by a wooden electricity pole and lovely pine tree). The main direction of this track is north, but it has several bends as it meanders through cultivation and past some lovely properties, with a fine view to the Bay of Sant Antoni. Ignore the concrete lane to Can Tono d'en Real. You pass villas called Can Sabina and Can Belize, then more *fincas* and villas. Ignore the turn-off left to Casa Colina.

Soon you come to a signpost for a **mountain bike route, MTB8** (4h), which runs left to Cala Tarida and right down to Sant Antoni. Our direction is to the left; the walk to Sant Antoni is longer and not as pretty.

As soon as you turn left on MTB8 your main direction is west. But again you will negotiate many bends. Now ascending, follow MTB8, ignoring the dead-end sign. You pass some nice old *fincas.* The track becomes a path and runs alongside some lovely old stone walls. Then the cultivated land ends and the route runs through the woods, still ascending.

When you meet another **MTB8 signpost**, the route heads south for a while. Then path widens out and descends. Soon you can see the sea and the white houses on the coast. There are old terraces on the right, now sadly abandoned. Another signpost points you along the route and the next sign tells you to ignore a turn-off to the right.

Soon the path leads into a track (where a huge villa was under construction at time of writing; **5h**). This track leads into another, where the Torrent de sa Fontassa is to the left. There are **three MTB8 signposts** in quick succession here (the photo above shows one of them); follow these signs. You pass an old *finca* on the left called Can Behant and, later, a white *finca.* Finally you reach the asphalt road. Turn right on the road for a short distance, then leave it by turning left on a green/white waymarked path. This leads you to **Cala Tarida** (**6h**), with its beach, restaurants and bus stop.

Walk 8: FROM SANT JOAN TO PORTINATX

Distance: 12km/7.4mi; 4h

Grade: moderate, with two short ascents and a long descent of 200m/650ft; the narrow coastal path demands careful footwork.

Equipment: stout shoes or walking boots, swimwear, picnic, water; see also page 10 (top). Those of you with a sense of adventure, who would like to tackle some of the old overgrown paths from Cala d'en Serra, should take long trousers; see page 61.

How to get there: Cala de Sant Vicent 🚌 from Eivissa into Sant Joan, or Portinatx 🚌 to the Sant Joan turn-off 1km outside the village
To return: 🚌 from Portinatx to Eivissa

Short walk: From Portinatx use the map to follow the coastal path in the opposite direction from the main walk, and turn back along the same path when you come to the lighthouse (4km/2.5mi; 1h15min; easy, but you must walk carefully on the narrow coastal path; or 🚌 to and from Portinatx).

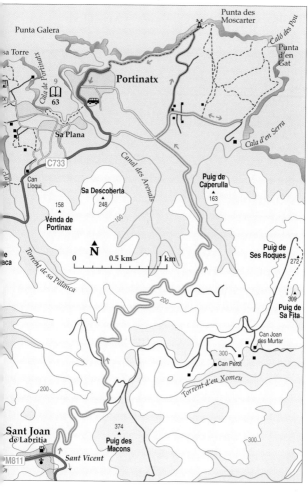

Thid his walk follows a high-level country road which, although asphalted, sees little traffic. There are magnificent views across cultivation towards Cala d'en Serra.

Start the walk at the turn-off to Sant Joan and follow the PM811 into the village (**10min**). Keep on the PM811 through **Sant Joan**, passing the **church**. At the end of the village the PM811 bends right: leave it here, heading left (north) on an asphalted country road. Climbing gently, ignore all turn-offs left and right. On the right are hillsides and to the left a deep valley, rich in vegetation. The Talaia de Sant Joan with its transmitter rises in the west.

After climbing east, the lane begins to descend. In the far distance, to the left, you can see the road to Portinatx, while the lighthouse you will visit later is

Cala d'en Serra

visible in the north. Soon you're descending in zigzags. Ten minutes later an unsurfaced road marked 'Privado' (closed to motorists) forks off right (**1h**); it goes via Puig de ses Roques to Puig de sa Fita. (This latter, a 309m/1015ft-high mountain with a beautiful panorama, is also called Rey. If you want to climb it, allow an *additional* 2h.)

Some 20 minutes later, ignore a track off right; keep to the road, which makes a long drawn-out curve to the left (north-northwest). But four-five minutes later *do* fork right: take the asphalt road downhill. This is the country road connecting Portinatx and Cala d'en Serra. As you curve to the right you pass house No 29 — a pretty, isolated *finca*. Then you head east. Soon you're looking deep into **Cala d'en Serra** (**2h**). The ruins of a hotel that was never completed have sadly disfigured this coastal landscape for many years.

(*Intrepid pathfinders may like to find their way to the lighthouse by following the coast from here — via Punta d'en Gat, Caló des Pou and Punta des Moscarter. There's also another route along the old walls to the lighthouse. Both routes are overgrown and have a touch of adventure, but don't attempt them without the 1:25,000 Cala de Portinatx map (773-I), a compass and/or GPS ... to say nothing of long trousers.*)

Those of you out for a walk rather than a battle with undergrowth will be happy to know there is an easier way to Ibiza's north coast. Walk back west along the road the way you came. Pass the house with the two blue stones at the entrance (on the left). Ignore the turn-off right by the electricity pole. Then the road runs through a fenced-in area. You pass a yellow villa on the left and cross a track. Where the road turns left, you see villa No 29 on the right. Leave the asphalt road at this point, turning right (north) on a rough track.

Shortly after turning you'll see Casa Claudia on the right, and some blue triangles — confirming that you are on the right track. Keep left at a fork. Very shortly afterwards meet the **coastal path** (**3h**), which you will later follow to the left. But first go right, to the **lighthouse**, then return the same way.

From the lighthouse follow the narrow, blue-marked coastal path west-southwest for about 2km, making sure to follow the blue waymarks at all the forks. Once in **Portinatx** (**4h**), take the road up to the bus stop — but not before having a swim and a good meal.

Walk 9: FROM PORTINATX TO CALA XARRACA

See also photograph on page 112
Distance: 12km/7.4mi; 4h30min
Grade: fairly strenuous, with overall ascents/descents of 100m/330ft
Equipment: stout shoes or walking boots, picnic, water, swimwear; see also page 10 (top)
How to get there: 🚌 from Eivissa to Portinatx
To return: 🚌 from Cala Xarraca to Eivissa (Portinatx bus)
Short walk: Portinatx — Punta sa Torre — Portinatx. Follow the main walk to the Torre de Portinatx and then to Punta sa Torre (45min). Then retrace your steps (4km/2.5mi; 1h35min; quite easy).

This walk takes you along coastal paths, through woods and cultivation. There are some fine coastal rock formations on view, as well as a watchtower.

Begin the walk at the **bus stop** in **Portinatx**. Walk southwest down the paved path behind the beach. Then climb the coastal path; it's also paved at first. You come to a second beach (**Petit Arenal**). Pass some boat-houses, then climb up to a fence. Further on you can easily get over the fence where it's been trampled underfoot. Cross over a low wall and rise up through a little wood, only a few metres from the cliff-edge (photograph on page 112). The path rises to a small plateau and then an asphalt lane (**20min**). Follow the lane to the right uphill, then turn right towards Club Portinatx. Keep straight ahead on the track towards the watchtower (which you can see from here); don't turn left on the lane which becomes blocked off by a fence. Soon you're at the **Torre de Portinatx** (**30min**).

On leaving the tower, walk back the way you came for 100m/yds, then turn left (northeast) on a good

Rock arch at Punta sa Torre, west of Portinatx (Walk 9)

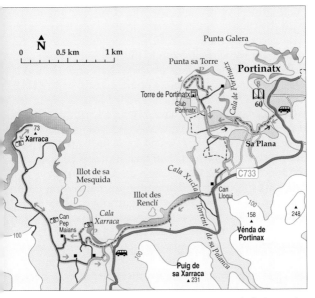

gravel track. At a private entrance, turn left into the woods. Three-four minutes later, head right downhill to the sea on a steep path. Walk left along the bright-white karst at **Punta sa Torre**; in two minutes you come to the impressive **rock arch** shown opposite. Continue southwest for a few minutes, to some large rocks, a pleasant picnic spot (**45-50min**; Picnic 9a).

It's a pity that we can't just continue along the coast from here, but unfortunately part of the old coastal path in this area has become too eroded in recent years to be used. So climb back up the path you descended (other paths further west are usually blocked by fencing). Retrace your steps past Club Portinatx and walk on to the main road (C733). Not far before the C733, at another junction, turn right on a dirt track. The track runs parallel with the C733 and then bends left to join the main road (just by Can Lloquí restaurant and mini-golf). Use the walkway alongside the **C733** for just 100m/yds — only to where it bends left (**1h25min**). At this point take the slightly overgrown path that zigzags down to the coast; for much of the time you're beside a water pipe. (There is also a wide track down to the beach another 250m further along the road.)

In under 10 minutes the path takes you to **Cala Xuclà** (**1h35min**). From here climb west over the coastal rocks on a path waymarked with red metal posts.

At the fork five minutes past the cove, take the lower path, by the sea. Soon you are above a small bay, with easy access to the sea. A little later you come to the restaurant Renclí facing out to the little Illot des Renclí. Follow the lane leading to the restaurant for about 40m/yds, and then continue on the coastal path. (Take care as you walk along the cliff-edge here — there are two places where you'll have a bit of a scramble. Climb down steps to some boathouses and later cross a stony cove. At the end of it, steps take you back up. You pass an impressive villa and then take more steps down to the sandy beach at **Cala Xarraca (2h35min)**.

Cross the beach and continue on the coastal path. You come to a **tiny cove with boathouses (2h50min**; Picnic 9b). Just before the boathouses the ongoing path climbs steeply up the hillside. (It's quite eroded; you could just stay on the lane and refer to the map to get to the top.) Once on the top, follow the slightly overgrown path south, quickly meeting a good crossing track (**3h**), where you head right. Keep on this track through light pine woods and, when you come to a track 'roundabout' go right (north). After about 80m, watch on your left for a path which will be your route when you return from the viewpoint ahead. In a couple of minutes you come to cultivated terraces with olive, almond, carob and fig trees. A minute later head right on a path; it takes you to a beautiful **viewpoint** at the cliff-edge, from where you look back along the whole coast to Portinatx. Return from here to the main track and follow it back to the path 80m before the 'round-about' (now on your *right*). Follow this path uphill to an old white *finca*, **Can Pep Maians (3h20min)**.

Follow the access road away from the farm, curving right (west) and, when you come to a T-junction, turn right. Now a lovely high-level track takes you towards the sea (north-northwest), past some cultivated terraces on the left. Once in a while, through breaks in the trees, you can see the lighthouse. Ignore a track off left some five minutes along. When you come to a plantation, the track forks; keep right (there is soon a stone wall on your right. A bay, **Es Caló des Porcs**, twinkles below on your left. At the next fork (with another track 'round-about'), keep left downhill. The track ends above the cliffs (**3h45min**), where steps lead down to the sea.

Turn back here, past the track running in from the right, the cultivated terraces (now on your right) and access road to Can Pep Maians (left). Some 150m/yds past the turn-off to Can Pep, take the next turn-off left. Follow this track down into the valley, heading east towards the C733. Go through a gap in a dry-stone wall and past a property. Cross a dirt track and walk between some cultivated terraces. Seven-eight minutes after joining this track you come to a lane: turn left and follow it north, passing some beautiful villas (one is called Can Xarraca). You can cut off a bend in the lane two minutes along, rejoining it by a transformer building. Back at **Cala Xarraca**, follow the lane up to the **bus stop** on the C733 (**4h30min**).

The coastal path between Cala Xuclà and Cala Xarraca

Walk 10: TORRE DES MOLAR FROM PORT DE SANT MIQUEL

Distance: 4km/2.5mi; 1h30min

Grade: easy, with overall ascents/descents of about 150m/500ft

Equipment: stout shoes, swimwear; see also page 10 (top)

How to get there and return: 🚌 from Eivissa to/from Port de Sant Miquel, or 🚗

This short walk takes you to magnificent viewpoints over the north coast. Your goal is an old watchtower with a viewing platform. There are three chances to swim — at Cala des Multons, on the south side of the Illa des Bosc peninsula, and at Cala de Sant Miquel.

Begin the walk at the bus stop at **Port de Sant Miquel**: walk past the parking area to **Cala de Sant Miquel**. Then climb the coastal path on the west side of the cove (blue waymarks). When you come to the kiosk at **Cala des Multons** (**5min**; Picnic 10), take the narrow footpath up the streambed. The path bends right and crosses the valley. You climb the north side of the ridge, with the streambed on your left, and come to a ruined house. Here the path kinks to the right, runs a short way back down the valley, then bends left to a wide gravel track (**17min**).

Follow this access drive to the right uphill, to a villa on a high ridge, where the track ends. From the garage of the villa take a faint path downhill, overlooking the mock watchtower on Illa des Bosc.  This slightly-overgrown path quickly meets a good coastal path: head left (a right leads back to Cala des Multons), undulating to a fine **viewpoint** over the cliffs.

The blue waymarks then take you to a wide gravel track (also waymarked in blue); follow this to the right downhill. The Torre des Molar beckons now, from the other side of the valley. The track turns sharp right in the streambed, where you look down on an old house and some boathouses. Soon you can also see back into Cala de Sant Miquel. Then you're at the beach on the tiny **Illa des Bosc** peninsula.

Cala des Multons

66

Unfortunately, access to the peninsula itself is not possible — it's a private estate. So climb steeply back the way you came. At the hairpin bend in the streambed (**35min**) follow the blue-waymarked track steeply uphill. The gravel access track you were on earlier comes in from the left at a pass; this is your route later in the walk. For now keep uphill to a fork, then take the blue-waymarked track through a sprinkling of conifers to the well-preserved 18th-century **Torre des Molar** (**50min**). You enjoy a marvellous view down over rocky Illa Murada.

From here return to the hilltop where the track to the tower meets the gravel track (**58min**) and head left.

At the next fork, almost at once, go right (you came in from the left on this access track on your way up). Descend quite steeply into the valley, through a light wood. At the house that you passed earlier (**1h05min**) take the same path downhill that you climbed on the way up, back to **Port de Sant Miquel** (**1h30min**).

Cycle tour 2: SANT ANTONI • SANT RAFEL • SANT ANTONI

See route on the touring map; the start of the tour is also shown on plan of Sant Antoni on page 21.

Distance: 30km/18.6mi; 4h (15km/9.3; 2h in each direction)

Grade: moderate, with a long ascent of about 250m/820ft at the start and a shorter ascent of about 100m/330ft on the return

Equipment: picnic, water; see also page 14

How to get there: the tour starts and ends at Sant Antoni, but can be done in reverse from Sant Rafel; the trip must be done in both directions as the buses unfortunately do not take bikes.

Shorter tour: to the Coll des Rossellons and back (15km/9.3mi; 2h), with a single long ascent of about 250m/820ft

You'll see for yourself just how small Ibiza is, when you do this cycle tour across the island. Starting out from the west coast, you'll be in the capital in about two hours.

Start the tour at the harbourside in **Sant Antoni**. Ride south on the promenade up to the mouth of the river **Es Regueró**. Then turn left and cross the main road to Sant Josep (PM803). On your left is the Regueró Valley. The lane, with little traffic, will follow this stream for some kilometres (ignore all turn-offs). Vines and almond trees are the most prominent crop around here. In the distance a mast marks the summit of Sa Talaiassa (Walk 7). The lane climbs slightly to the southeast, distancing itself from the streambed. Keep straight ahead on **Camí Ramal de Benimussa**, curving gently uphill through carob and almond trees, past a water tank and then a pretty villa on the left. Once

you've crossed a dirt track, the now-deep valley is close by on your left.

Eventually, the lane moves further away from the valley, and you come to a T-junction with another asphalt lane (about 6km). Turn left here, passing a **pumping station**. You are now on **Cycle route 19**.

Sant Rafel

The Molí des Puig d'en Valls: as soon as roadworks on the C731 are completed, it will be possible to continue the tour via this lovely windmill (see the touring map) and carry on to Cala Talamanca.

The fields are gradually giving way to woods, and the climb is somewhat steeper. You pass a fenced-in property on the right. On the left there is a fine view over to Puig Nunó, and the Serra Grossa rises in a mighty upthrust in front of you. You cycle through cultivated terraces, with the Regueró Valley still on your left. At a fork, Cycle route 19 turns right to Eivissa; you keep left here, following the direction indicated by a green and yellow-painted stone showing a heart pierced by an arrow, pointing the way to the 'Casita Verde'. This road rises to the **Coll des Rossellons** (246m/800ft; about 9km).

Another valley, the **Torrent des Fornas**, greets you on the far side of this pass, as you follow the lane east-northeast downhill past more terraces. After about 3.5km, where an unsurfaced track goes right, the lane turns left to cross the stream. Turn left here, cross the *torrent*, and climb a bit on the far side. Now cycling east on asphalt, you can soon see the Botafoc lighthouse off to your right. You pass a church on the right and then take the first turning right to the main C731 (at KM5.5), just south of the centre of **Sant Rafel**.

At time of writing there were roadworks here on the main road, so it's best to turn back now and retrace your route via the **Coll des Rossellons** to **Sant Antoni**.

Walk 11: BAYS WEST OF SANT ANTONI

Distance: 6.5km/4mi; 2h35min

Grade: easy, with overall ascents/descents of just 50m/160ft

Equipment: lightweight walking boots or shoes with good grip, picnic, water, swimwear; see also page 10 (top)

How to get there: 🚌 or ⛴ from Sant Antoni to Cala Bassa (the bus is cheaper, but the boat ride is more fun).

To return: 🚌 or ⛴ from Cala Codolar to Sant Antoni

Short walk: Follow the main walk to Platjes de Comte (3km/2mi; 1h10min) and return by bus back to Sant Antoni.

Ibiza's picturesque west coast is explored on this walk, where you discover steep cliffs and pretty sandy bays. As long as there is a light breeze, you won't be uncomfortably hot, even in summer.

Begin the walk in **Cala Bassa** by walking to the west end of the bay and climbing a stony path which overlooks **Cala de Sant Antoni** and the town's hotels. The main path turns away from the coast (**15min**) and begins to go downhill. (At this point sure-footed walkers could continue along a coastal path. It ends at Cap de la Bassa. After that just follow the coastal rocks across the cape, with fine views. When you get to Cala Roig rejoin the main walk path. This alternative takes 20 minutes.) Soon you look down into another bay, **Cala Roig**. In the distance you can see an old watchtower and, beyond it, yet another tower — the lighthouse on the offshore island of Sa Conillera. This stretch of coast is little frequented, even at the height of summer, and the high plateau offers a choice of picnic spots in sun or shade (Picnic 11).

As you continue along the coast, with the sea on your right, take care not to walk too close to the edge: the breakers have worn away and undercut the cliffs in places, and it's always possible that a section of cliff-edge could give way. No matter what the season, you can enjoy solitude along this gorgeous stretch of coast, even though a busy beach is not far away.

Soon the watchtower and the

On this walk you look out across deeply-etched coves towards Es Vedrà.

lighthouse beyond it are aligned (**30min**). You come onto an unsurfaced road but leave it again after a few minutes, to make your own way to the right, down to a **boathouse**, which you reach four minutes later. Take a swim in the crystal-clear water, then continue to the watchtower, the **Torre d'en Rovira** (**45min**), from where you look across to the next bay, Cala Conta.

Start back from the watchtower along the track you took to reach it. Once you have left the little wood there are more fine, open views across the bay. After about 300m/yds, you reach the unsurfaced road at a 'round-about' and turn right, edging the wood. After another 300m/yds, when this motorable track turns left, continue half-right on a pretty little path running through pines, heading straight for the sea (some blue-painted metal posts mark the path). Soon you're following the coastal path to the left, looking down into the busy bay of Platjes de Comte. Opposite are the uninhabited islands of Bosc, Espart, Gorra, Baxell and Plana, facing you across a stretch of sea. There's another opportunity for a swim now, at **Platjes de Comte** (also called 'Cala Conta'; **1h10min**).

From here continue south, taking a track round landward side of some villas. You skirt an lovely palm-ringed villa, Ca'n Embarcador, and then an Arabian-looking estate, Villa Punta Embarcador. Several more

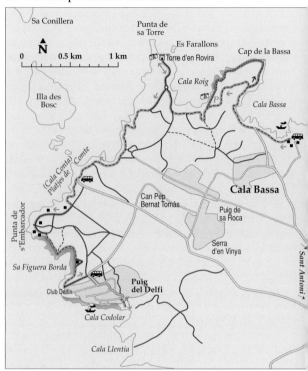

little 'palaces' follow, but unfortunately the track runs behind these imposing properties before you are able to head back to the sea.

Then you circle two stony beaches before detouring behind another group of houses. (There *is* a narrow path between the cliff-edge and the fenced-off private land here, but it is very exposed.) The next landmark is a long row of terraced bungalows running down to the sea, **Club Delfin**. You come on to a tarred road just before the bungalows (with the bus stop for your return), and from the reception follow the road to the left (marked 'Beach') through the resort of **Puig del Delfin**.

Soon you're just above **Cala Codolar**; steps take you down to the beach (**2h25min**) — your last chance for a swim along the walk. It's a ten-minute walk from the beach back to the **bus stop** (**2h35min**), from where you can get a bus to Sant Antoni. In high season you can also take a boat.

Walk 12: THE COASTAL PATH TO CALA SALADA

Distance: 9km/5.6mi; 3h

Grade: easy, with overall ups and downs of 80m/260ft, but you must be sure-footed for a couple of scrambles into *calas*.

Equipment: lightweight walking boots or shoes with good grip, picnic, water, swimwear; see also page 10 (top)

How to get there: 🚌 to Sant Antoni

To return: 🚕 taxi from the restaurant at Cala Salada, then 🚌 from Sant Antoni

Short walk: Follow the main walk as far as you like — perhaps to Punta de sa Galera — and return the same way.

On this walk you'll be following the coastal path to the bays north of Sant Antoni. There are several spots where you can go for a swim, and the sea breezes ensure that it's not too hot, even in summer — but remember that there is little shade on the coastal path.

Start the walk at the **bus stop** in **Sant Antoni** (see town plan on page 21). Follow the promenade to **Caló des Moro**. From here you will take the coastal path; it is waymarked with blue triangles and green/white paint. But the green and white waymarks lead inland from Punta de sa Galera, so be sure to follow the blue triangles from there!

Once at Caló des Moro, walk along the gravel road, which quickly peters out into a narrow coastal path beside the sea. Beyond the small point called **Roca Baixa**, you pass a little aquarium with a bar. Sometimes the path edges the cliffs, but the route is protected with wooden fencing. The path cuts across a small peninsula, **Cap Blanc**. You need to be sure-footed just before the tiny sandy cove, **Cala Gració**. Cross this busy beach and pick up the path again, passing some boathouses and then crossing an even smaller cove. Follow the blue and white/green waymarks, staying on the coastal path just beside the sea, with a wall up to your right. *Ignore* the track with green waymark posts; it leads inland. Be careful not to trip up on the rough karst surface here — it's real ankle-twisting terrain. The path rounds the seaside of a walled-in **desalination plant with a small recreation park,**an idea spot for a picnic (**1h**; Picnic 12).

The path heads straight for a white villa with a red roof high up on the **Cap Negret** cliffs, with wonderful coastal views. You pass this villa on the sea side and, shortly afterwards, walk below a small restaurant with a terrace. Past here, the path again runs very close to the cliff-edge (where you may notice some boundary markers). About 300m/yds beyond the clifftop villa steps on the left invite you down for a swim. There are several older buildings in typical Ibizan architectural style in this area. Round forms predominate, and they are generally much more attractive than the more recently-built concrete villas. Soon you have fine views to the slender promontory of Punta de sa Galera — its cliffs particularly striking when seen in the afternoon sun. (It's worth following the rocky path to the end of this point.)

You meet a motorable track at **Punta de sa Galera**, but *don't* follow it inland; *ignore* the green/white

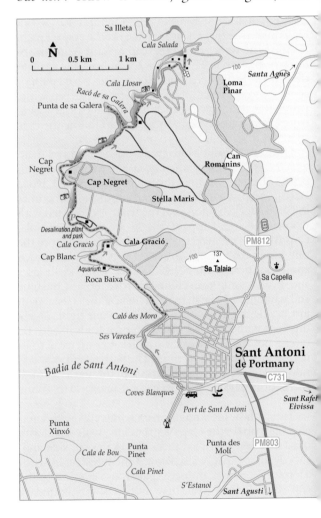

View to Sa Galera, with fishermen's boathouses in the foreground and Puig Nunó (255m) in the background

waymarks. Walk about 25m/yds to the left, and go through a gap in a wall. Take the *steep, skiddy path* down to a pebbly little cove, the **Racó de sa Galera**. Cross the tiny beach, then climb the steps up towards a villa. The coastal path continues left below the villa and ends at a huge green iron gate. Two stone posts mark the path down to **Cala Llosar (2h30min)**. There have been landslides around here; keep away from any roped-off areas. The bizzare rock formations are a wonderful place to take a break but, if you decide to swim, watch out for sea urchins — and for young naturists who love to sunbathe on the flat rocks.

To continue to Cala Salada follow the old road uphill, past a car park on the right and inland from some villas. Ignore a track to a transformer building on the left. At the next junction turn left on a road, with villas on both sides. Don't miss your small path to the left after the last villa — *watch for the blue waymark*, near a green fence. This path takes you down through the wood to another road, where you turn right. Turn left before a tennis court, then take the steps at the left of a transformer building, down to the restaurant at **Cala Salada (3h)**. Enjoy a swim and a meal at the restaurant and, when you are ready to head back to base, ask the waiter to call a taxi. It will arrive in about 15 minutes, and in the same time you'll be back in **Sant Antoni**.

Walk 13: SANTA AGNES • PENYA ESBARRADA • SANTA AGNES

See also photograph on pages 6-7

Distance: 6km/3.7mi; 2h30min

Grade: fairly easy, with ascents/descents of 150m/500ft, but you must be sure-footed and have a head for heights.

Equipment: lightweight walking boots or shoes with good grip, water; see also page 10 (top)

How to get there and return: ⛍ from Eivissa or Sant Antoni to/from Santa Agnès (high season only), or ⛍ (park about 1.5km along, before the walk turns off to the right).

Short walk: Follow the main walk to the viewpoint/restaurant (40min), then go back the same way to Santa Agnès (3km/2mi; 1h20min; easy).

This walk in the lonely northwest corner of the island takes you to a remarkable coastal landscape and then over the Penya Esbarrada — where you'll enjoy that invigorating feeling of being in high mountains. This is probably one of the finest walk on Ibiza.

Start the walk by heading west from the restaurant Can Cosmí. Follow the little-used lane signed 'Camí d'es Pla de Corona' (blue triangle waymarks); ignore all turn-offs. Heading for the high coastal hills, after about 1.5km you pass a couple of *fincas*. Just 100m/yds further on, the lane curves left by an old stone building (where motorists could park). Leave the lane here: descend a track at the left of a wall *(not waymarked)*. You look towards some impressive rock formations on the coastal cliffs, with the islands of Ses Margalides rising in front of you (**40min**; Picnic 13). To the left is a **viewpoint** and the small **Puertas del Cielo restaurant**.

From here head north, then west, on a path way-marked with red and blue arrows. Descending steeply towards the sea, keep right at a fork four minutes down (more arrows). You look down to a rocky cove and the

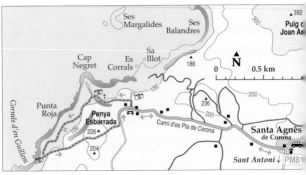

76

The Camí d'es Pla de Corona edges a huge agricultural plateau

Cap Negret promontory. Now you see two other rocks out to sea, Es Corrals and Sa Illot. The rock walls to your left, **Penya Esbarrada**, are reminiscent of the Dolomites. The path improves as it descends through a wood, straight towards the vertical rock wall. Ignore a turn-off right to some cultivated seaside terraces.

Now you come upon two exposed stretches of path, where you must tread *very carefully*. Once the path has crossed a rock barrier, you look out to Sa Conillera island with its lighthouse. The tree-capped summit in front of you is Puig Nunó (255m/835ft). Keep right at a fork (**1h05min**) and descend towards the **ruined farm** below on the hillside. Take a rest at these old ruins, where you will find a **domed oven** built into one of the drystone walls. The waymarks now take you past abandoned terraces and an old **water deposit** (with the number '20' in faded red paint). Soon you're walking alongside a wall, through thick fennel bushes. (If you don't suffer from vertigo, you could walk on the wall.)

At the end of the wall the path climbs steeply back uphill. Soon another **viewpoint** overlooks the bay called **Corrals d'en Guillem**. At a junction of several paths (**1h25min**), head left (northeast) uphill, to cross the 200m/650ft-high ridge of Penya Esbarrada. *Watch for the arrow waymarks* — now pointing back the way you came. You pass an **old well** and later a **lime kiln**; then the way levels out in a wood. Once you've crossed over the ridge, head gently downhill. You're quickly back on the **Camí d'es Pla de Corona** (**1h50min**), about 300m/yds south of where you left it. Follow the lane back to **Santa Agnès** (**2h30min**).

Walk 14: FROM SANTA EULARIA TO CALA LLONGA

See also photograph on page 29   **Distance:** 8km/5mi; 2h30min

Grade: fairly strenuous, with overall ascents/descents of 200m/650ft; you must be sure-footed on short sections of path beyond La Torre

Equipment: lightweight walking boots, long trousers, swimwear, picnic, water; see also page 10 (top)

How to get there: 🚌 to Santa Eulària (or ⛴)
To return: 🚌 or ⛴ from Cala Llonga

Short walk: If you want to avoid the strenuous climb, then go only as far as the villa La Torre on Punta Blanca and return to Santa Eulària the same way (6km/3.7mi; 1h45min).

For most of the way this walk follows an ancient, high-level footpath. Although the route is now waymarked (dark blue triangles), as often as not you will walk in total solitude between one tourist centre and another.

Begin the walk at the **bus station** in **Santa Eulària**: walk down to the sea and turn right (southwest) on the promenade. At the end of the promenade, looking right, there's a good view of Santa Eulària's old church on the Puig de Missa. Pass the hotels Mar Sol and Río Mar on their seaward side and come to the mouth of the **Riu de Santa Eulària**. Cross it about 100m upstream, via the attractive bridge shown opposite. Then turn left on the promenade (Carrer des Rhododendres, then Carrer ses Violetes). Shortly afterwards, you pass the setting for Picnic 14.

Several walkways head inland on both sides of the river. Take the paved walkway uphill and then down to the sea, where there's a pleasant beach (**Caló de d'Alga**). Soon the Siesta resort is behind you.

Now follow the blue-waymarked coastal path; it begins by the **massive cairn** shown on page 81. The pretty path delves into a little pine wood, and soon you meet a fork: keep left, to continue along the coast. Follow the blue triangles. Another fork is met a minute later; again, keep left — close to the edge of the cliffs. Just past **Punta de s'Aguait** (Picnic 16), the path meets a wide dirt track waymarked with blue-painted metal poles as well as blue triangles, which you follow to the left. You pass the villa La Ventana and climb a little, ignoring all the small paths which turn off left to the coast and staying on this wide track. About now a recently-built defence tower comes into view to the south. It belongs to the villa La Torre, which stands on Punta Blanca; sometimes a flag is flying there. Ignore the concrete lane branching left some 12 minutes along

— it would only take you to a small villa called Es Baladres. (There is also another lane to this farm 20m/yds further on.) Continue along the track you are on, a short uphill section of which is concreted. Five minutes later you find yourself high above the sea, heading south. Ignore a right turn to a ruined house. Not far past this turn, at a fork, keep left downhill on the access track to La Torre (the track to the right is followed on Walk 16). At this precise point you can't see La Torre, but you will see it after about 50m/yds.

Then, about 100m/yds before the entrance gate to **La Torre**, turn right on a footpath. *(The Short walk turns back here.)* You climb the coastal cliffs, where you walk close to the cliff-edge. Below lies a pebbly beach, Cala Blanca, with no sand at all. In the valley you can see the entrance to a tunnel —

the only access to Cala Blanca unless you come by boat. When the path runs into a streambed (**1h10min**), the walk will continue by climbing up the valley. But first turn left to the edge of the cliffs and follow the path downhill and through the **tunnel** to **Cala Blanca**. You won't need a torch. You can scramble down to the stony beach if you like, and swim if the sea isn't too rough.

The pebble beach at Cala Blanca (right) can only be reached on foot or by boat; below: the graceful bridge over the Riu de Santa Eulària

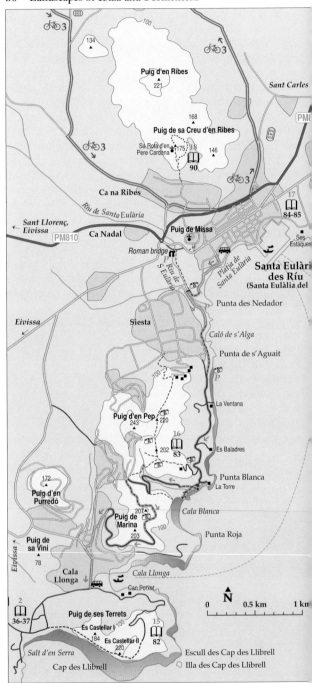

Massive cairn marking the start of the coastal path south of Santa Eulària

Now go back through the tunnel and walk just a short way to the right, to the mouth of the *torrent* (be careful; there is a sudden, steep drop to the sea). Enjoy the magnificent scenery of rocks and sea. Then climb west-northwest up the valley on a beautiful path through thick vegetation. The path widens to a **cart track**, climbing in deep bends. Ignore a turn-off to the left after seven-eight minutes. Five minutes later you reach a **road junction**. Take the footpath a few metres/yards to the left (marked by a blue metal pole), going south uphill past a little **water deposit** on the left.

As you climb to the top of **Puig de Marina**, ignore all turn-offs left and right; follow the waymarking. You pass a caved-in **lime kiln**. This superb footpath will take you up to 207m/680ft. On the right you look out over cultivated fields in the valley, on the left you catch glimpses of the sea through the trees. Soon you have a beautiful view over the cove at Salt d'en Serra (Cycle tour 2 and Walk 15) and, shortly after, you cross the highest point, marked by another high cairn.

On the descent, which may be difficult for walkers who are not sure-footed, follow the red and blue triangle waymarks carefully. The path runs along the left-hand side of the hill, descending steeply. Take care: in places it has been badly damaged by moto-cross riders. When you come to an unmarked fork, keep right. The path meets a wide dirt track by another blue-painted metal pole. Follow this downhill (less steeply). Soon you look left down into the fjord-like bay of Cala Llonga. When you reach the hotels, the track is asphalted. Make your way down to the beach at **Cala Llonga**, where you will find the **bus stop** (**2h30min**).

Walk 15: PUIG DE SES TERRETS

Distance: 8km/5mi; 3h

Grade: fairly strenuous, with some steep ascents/descents of about 300m/1000ft overall, but you must be sure-footed and have a head for heights on the descent (or retrace your steps to return)

Equipment: lightweight walking boots or stout shoes, swimwear, picnic, water; see also page 10 (top)

How to get there and return: 🚌 to/from Cala Llonga

This walk leads you to spot with overwhelming views and some excavations. Although the walk is fairly short, I suggest you allow a whole day, relaxing at Cala Salt d'en Serra and Cala Llonga.

Start the walk from the **bus stop** at **Cala Llonga** beach. Follow the wide track uphill to the east, passing **Can Porxet**. The track climbs through bends up to 200m, then ends. Now follow the path further uphill. The **Puig de ses Terrets** has two summits: Es Castellar II (220m) and Es Castellar I (184m). The excavations are on **Es Castellar II** and are soon reached (**1h**). Be careful around here: don't try to go into the ruins, just look at them from above.

Experienced walkers can carry on to the western summit, **Es Castellar I** (**2h**), and from there *slowly and*

carefully, keeping well clear of the edge of the cliff, follow the cliff-side path down to **Cala Salt d'en Serra**. From the restaurant, take the wide track back to **Cala Llonga** (**3h**).

Instituto Geográfico pillar atop Es Castellar

Walk 16: PUIG D'EN PEP

See also photographs on pages 79 and 81

Distance: 9km/5.6mi; 3h

Grade: easy, but you must be sure-footed on the steep descent from the summit; overall ascent/descent of 220m/720ft

Equipment: lightweight walking boots, water; see also page 10 (top)

How to get there and return: 🚌, 🚢 or 🚗 to/from Santa Eulària

Short walk: as Walk 14, page 78

This walk takes you up the 220m/725ft-high Puig d'en Pep near Santa Eulària. You enjoy the sweetly-scented solitude of the woods and some splendid views.

Begin the walk in the centre of Santa Eulària: follow the main road west (Carrer de Sant Jaume; see plan on page 21). Where the road turns right, branch off left to the Roman bridge (photograph page 90). Then take the cobbled walkway to the bridge shown on page 79, cross it, and head along the promenade to the Siesta resort at **Caló de s'Alga**. The coastal path begins at the massive cairn shown on page 81; from here follow the notes for Walk 14 on page 78. There are lovely picnic places at **Punta de s'Aguait** (Picnic 16). Keep following Walk 14 until it forks down left towards La Torre on Punta Blanca (**1h**). Then you head west uphill.

Climb the motorable track to the right here, heading steeply uphill. The route is waymarked with blue poles, blue triangles and red paint. Soon there are fine views to the right along the coast as far as the hills of Cala de Sant Vicent. Later you look down left into the fjord-like bay of Cala Llonga. When the **wide track abruptly ends** in front of the ochre-coloured villa Can Puig d'en Pep (under 15 minutes uphill), pick up a path to the right, waymarked in red and green/white, and with a sign prohibiting litter.

83

This path circumnavigates the villa, then rejoins the original path that was destroyed when the villa was built. A cairn and a red waymark show the ongoing direction of the path along the ridge. In two minutes the path bends away from the crest, heads right and levels out for a while. Shortly after it again runs along the crest, climbing gradually. You soon have a splendid view to Santa Eulària and Tago Mago. As you walk along the ridge, you look over left to Puig de Marina.

Soon you come to an important fork. The path to the left runs down to Valverde and on to Cala Llonga. Keep right and follow the path, to cross over the hills and head back towards Santa Eulària. The woodland path climbs again, past a stone marked 'Siesta'. At the next fork keep right. The path stays on the heights, and you reach a first summit (202m/660ft), where a large circular clearing invites you to take a break. Then you head gently northeast downhill. The deep blue sea twinkles through the green pines. On the left, through the trees, you look at the flat cultivation behind Cala Llonga. Ignore a steep turn-off down left; a minute later you're on the true summit of **Puig d'en Pep** (220m/720ft; **2h**) — although it is not the highest point in these hills. (The high point, at 243m, lies to the west of the path.) The view to the left is especially beautiful, while to the right, breaks in the trees lead the eye as far as Cala Boix.

Eventually you come to another fork, clearly marked with a red arrow, where you turn left. (The path straight ahead ends at some villas; if you find yourself above a garage roof, go back to the path!) Red arrows lead you down the steep path, until you reach an asphalt lane at a white house. From here just make your way seawards — perhaps via Edificio Brillant, Carrer ses Dalies and Carrer Margalides. At house No 47 you can take the narrow lane back to the promenade at Siesta. From there retrace your outgoing route back to **Santa Eulària** (**3h**).

Walk 17: FROM SANTA EULARIA TO ES CANAR

Distance: 7km/4.3mi; 2h15min
Grade: easy, with ascents/descents of under 50m/165ft overall
Equipment: lightweight shoes, water, swimwear; see also page 10 (top)
How to get there: 🚌 or ⛴ to Santa Eulària
To return: 🚌 or ⛴ from Es Canar
Short walk: Follow the main walk for as long as you like, and return the same way.

This delightful coastal walk takes you through coppices of pines and past a string of pretty coves to Es Canar. The reddish-brown colouring of the coastal rocks is seen at its best when the sun is low.

Begin along the seaside promenade in **Santa Eulària**: head left (northeast), past the **pier** and the **marina**. There's a beautiful old *finca* on the promenade that has not given way to modern buildings. Turn right in front of the hotel **Ses Estaques**, and follow the asphalt lane down to the sea. Pass the hotel and walk up the steep and stony coastal path that

Club Punta Arabí, passed near the end of the walk

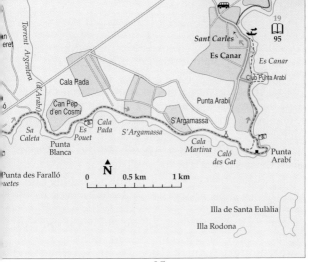

begins at the restaurant Ses Sabines. The path passes to the seaward side of all the villas and hotels, so at any forks, always head towards the sea. You rise quickly through a little pine wood, at the end of which you'll be enjoying wonderful views over the bay of Santa Eulària and neighbouring coves (**11min**; Picnic 17).

From this viewpoint you descend to the hotel **Ibiza Sol**, which can also be passed on the sea side (at least outside high season; in summer you *may* have to walk round it). Behind the hotel grounds you pick up the coastal path again. It runs above the reddish-brown coastal rocks. Continue through juniper and pines, past the Babylon Beach Bar down by the sea. Then the coastal path narrows and you walk between the cliff-edge and a wall with a fence on the top. (The sea has eaten up the narrow path in places along here, but it is only a metre down to the beach at this point, so wade if necessary. Wading is no problem if the sea is calm, but if the weather is stormy, you'll have to escape to the main road for a short way, then turn right at the Eroski supermarket and follow Carrer Colonia back to the coastal path.)

The path goes through a beautiful woodland area, which recently attracted the attention of hungry developers (**40min**). A minute later, a pretty stretch of sand

The stretch through pines at S'Argamassa, just beside the sea, is an especially beautiful park-like landscape.

comes into view, **Sa Caleta**. Six minutes later you have crossed this little beach with its Bora-Bora restaurant (in summer you'll have to fight your way through hordes of sun-bathers and swimmers). Then you cross the sand-filled mouth of the small **Torrent Argentera** (Torrent d'Arabí), beyond which there is also an upper and lower path; the lower path is walkable in fine weather.

Continue just by the coast. You'll have to duck down a couple of times, where low branches block the path, this small trail is in superb condition. Stretches of it go through private gardens; don't let that worry you; this is a public footpath. Soon you come to some **steps down to the sea (1h05min)** — time for a swim? Four-five minutes later pass a crumbled old **well**. The next beach en route (**Cala Pada**) is very busy in the summer. Continue through the lovely pine bosket shown above, at **S'Argamassa**. The next cove, **Cala Martina**, comes into view. In summer all these bays are packed out.

Beyond the Hotel Augusta and a campsite you come to the next cove, **Caló des Gat**, popular with naturists. You meet fewer people now. The path takes you over some cliffs, again through juniper and pines. To the right lie two small islands, Santa Eulària and Rodona. There are still wonderful coastal views ahead. Climb over a **wall (1h45min)**. The path is now on a **high plateau**, gently ascending and skirting to the sea side of some coastal properties. At **Club Punta Arabí (1h50min)** you have to turn left and head inland to the main road. Turn right, walk into **Es Canar** and continue to the **jetty (2h15min)** or to the **bus stop**, some 250m/yds further on.

Walk 18: SANTA EULARIA AND THE PUIG DE SA CREU D'EN RIBES

See also photograph on page 29   **Distance:** 5km/3mi; 2h
Grade: mostly an easy stroll, but you must be sure-footed for the ascent to and descent from the summit; the path is fairly steep, stony and slippery when wet; overall ascents/descents of about 200m/650ft
Equipment: lightweight walking boots, water; see also page 10 (top)
To get there and return: 🚌, ⛴ or 🚗 to/from Santa Eulària

Take plenty of time over this short walk, which introduces you to three of the oldest monuments on Ibiza — the lovely church shown below, the Roman bridge, and the chapel Sa Rota d'en Pere Cardona on Puig de sa Creu d'en Ribes (both illustrated overleaf). Wait for a fine, clear day to do this walk — there are superb views from the hilltop, even though you're only at 175m/575ft.

Begin the walk on the **promenade** in **Santa Eulària**, by heading southwest towards the river. The paved promenade soon ends and you continue past a couple of olive trees and hotels. As you walk towards the river, look up to the right, and you will see a beautiful bright-white church with an ochre dome on top of the hill; you visit it later in the walk.

When you come to the **Riu de Santa Eulària**, walk beside it on the pedestrian walkway, heading northwest up-river — not that there's much of a river during the

it's usually just a trickle. You quickly come to the **Roman bridge** (70AD) shown overleaf. Take a good look at this splendid ancient monument from all angles. Beyond the bridge the river is completely dry in summer, but oleander, reeds and fennel thrive down in the **riverbed** (**15min**; Picnic 18).

After taking a break, climb the stone steps on the right-hand side of the

The parish church on Puig de Missa was enlarged into a fortress in 1568.

river. The old Roman road takes you east to the town. Join the main road and follow it for a few metres, then climb the **signposted steps** up left to **Puig de Missa** and the church shown below. Once it was a mosque, and Islamic symbols can be seen on the dome. The building and the adjacent semicircular defence tower look more like a fortress than a church — hardly surprising, as it once served as one. Keen photographers will find subjects in plenty from this 100m/330ft-high viewpoint, with its fine panorama. Don't miss a visit to the little cemetery and the museum, before continuing the walk.

From up here on Puig de Missa you can see your next goal just in front of you: the green hill called Puig de sa Creu d'en Ribes. But from this angle trees obscure the tiny white chapel — also of Moorish origin — on its summit. To get there, refer to the plan on page 21: leave from the north side of the hill, cross straight over the main road (PM810), and turn left at the T-junction. Follow this road round to the right (north). At the next T-junction, the path is on the far side of the road, just to the left and indicated with brown signs. After four minutes it narrows and becomes quite steep. It goes through scrub and then zigzags up through a bit of wood with low trees. Take care on the ascent *and descent*.

The Arabic chapel/ shrine of Sa Rota d'en Pere Cardona atop the Puig de sa Creu d'en Ribes (top). Inside is a simple wooden cross and some tributes to miracle cures. Left: the Roman bridge at Santa Eulària (Picnic 18)

After a 10 minute climb you're just beside the tiny shrine/chapel, **Sa Rota d'en Pere Cardona**, just below the summit of the **Puig de sa Creu d'en Ribes (1h 10min)**. From here you enjoy more fine views over the town and the harbour.

From the summit there is a path ahead to a col; it then heads steeply east and then south, rejoining the main path. But it is sometimes overgrown. If so, it is best to simply retrace your steps back downhill to **Santa Eulària (2h)**.

Cycle tour 3: GARDENS AND WOODS NORTH OF SANTA EULARIA

See touring map; the first and last parts of the tour are shown in more detail on the walking map on page 80, and the roundabout where the tour begins on the town plan on page 21.

Distance: 14km/8.7mi; 1h30min

Grade: easy, with minimal ascents

Equipment: picnic, water; see also page 14

How to get there and return: cycle circuit based on Santa Eulària

This idyllic cycling circuit takes you along the intensively-cultivated flanks of the Puig de sa Creu d'en Ribes and the Puig d'Atzaró, past several attractive properties with drystone walls and old defence towers.

Start out on the northeast side of **Santa Eulària** (see plan on page 21), from the **roundabout** near the junction of Carrer Costa Ribas and the road to Sant Carles. Head northeast on the road on the north side of the roundabout. Keep left at a Y-fork (a right leads to the football ground). The road bends slightly left, and you soon leave the last houses of Santa Eulària behind, cycling past fields of reddish-brown earth, cultivated terraces with fig and carob trees, and some magnificent villas. Ignore all turn-offs, as you cycle to the right of the wooded **Puig d'en Ribes**.

At a crossroads with a track ahead (about 2.5km), turn left. You pass beside a large **reservoir** on your left. About 100m/yds past the end of the reservoir, turn right towards **Can Vidal**, an impressive property surrounded by a high wall and with a **mock defence tower**. Palms and banana trees grow here. Then a real, **old defence tower** pops up on the right. Ignore a turn-off to the right; keep ahead (northwest) on a track lined with drystone walls. At the next junction, head left (west) downhill. The tarred access lane to a *finca* comes in from the right behind you, and you immediately come to a T-junction: turn right here. The lane heads towards Puig d'Atzaró for a short time but, at a Y-fork, go left, to pass in front of another property, **Can Ramonet**.

Soon the famous old **defence tower at Balàfia** with its white rim is seen ahead in the distance (photograph page 27). Beyond a transformer building the lane goes back into woods. Go straight over the next two crossroads, and when you come to a T-junction, go left. This track then bends right immediately, to round the north side of the **Puig d'Atzaró**. On the left is the fertile

plain. You pass another beautiful **old defence tower** at **Can Jaumet** and then a building with a **white well**.

Behind **Can Mariano Mosson** turn left (north) on Camí Atzaró, an asphalt lane. You pass a beautiful house called Can Mariano Reco and soon meet the asphalt **country road between Balàfia and Es**

Above left: the old defence tower at Can Jaumet is reminiscent of the more famous one at Balàfia. Left and above: some of the landscapes that make this cycle tour such a joy, especially in springtime.

Figueral at a junction. Follow this to the left (west-northwest) for just 200m/yds.

Now, homeward bound, head southwest on a lane through vineyards and citrus gardens — making straight for the summit with the TV mast. The lane curves to the right (where Can Jaumet is straight ahead). Follow the lane in a long curve to the left. You pass a mini-market with a bar — a good place to take a break. Keep on this lane (south-southeast), ignoring all crossroads and turn-offs left and right.

Eventually (about 11km) the huge wall of the **reservoir** is off to the left. The lane curves right past Crazy Horse Farm, then climbs a bit, heading south. Soon you look right to **Puig d'en Pep**. At the next major junction keep left, heading southeast towards the sea. The **Puig de Missa** rises in front of you now, and shortly afterwards you're back in **Santa Eulària** (14km; **1h30min**).

Walk 19: FROM ES CANAR TO SANT CARLES

Distance: 8km/5mi; 2h45min

Grade: fairly strenuous, with an overall ascent of 350m/1150ft; you must be sure-footed for the descent into Cala Mastella

Equipment: walking boots, swimwear, water; see also page 10 (top)

How to get there: 🚌 or ⛴ to Es Canar

To return: 🚌 from Sant Carles

Short walk: End the walk at Cala Llenya or Club Playa Azul and return by boat or bus (2.5km/1.6mi; 55min).

This walk combines a coastal path with a hike through pine woods and cultivation. Another possibility is to follow it just to Sa Sení restaurant at Cala Mastella, then pick up Walk 23, continuing along the coastal path. When you get back to Cala Mastella, retrace your steps to Es Canar.

Start out at Es Canar: head north along the seaside promenade until the busy beach lies behind you. Pass some pines and continue along a good coastal path. Soon the next bay comes into view; this stretch of beach is behind you in four minutes and you come to another beach, **Punta Verde**, beyond which the path rises through pines. Even in summer you're unlikely to meet anyone here, only the occasional walker, so enjoy the solitude.

Pass to the inland side of the pretty **Las Perlas** apartments with all their greenery (**30min**). Follow the asphalt road a short way downhill, then turn right on the path back towards the sea, passing the Las Perlas swimming pool. Soon you're back on the cliffs, looking into another sandy cove. The path goes to the seaward side of the next apartments. Four minutes later you're at a small stony cove. Then, having walked uphill through pines, you reach **Cala Llenya (55min)**. In summer the sun-loungers are tightly packed together in this small bay, where space is at a premium. You can end the Short walk here by taking a boat back to Es Canar, Santa Eulària or Eivissa.

At the end of the bay, climb the second set of steps up towards the holiday villages Club Playa Azul and Can Jordi. From the top of the steps walk inland to the wide dirt track and turn right. The track quickly ends; follow the path downhill to the right. When you get to the bottom, turn sharp left (to the right are some **boathouses**). Now you climb steeply northeast, up a deeply-etched valley. At the top, keep the boundary wall of the Club Playa Azul on your right, and at the end of the wall keep straight ahead. You come into **Club Playa**

Azul (buses to Santa Eulària) via a small parking area, with a supermarket on your left.

Turn right on the road here and curve counter-clockwise a good halfway round the resort. At the **Azul Restaurant** fork right on an asphalt lane. Then, at the T-junction that follows, turn right (there is an old **threshing floor** on your left at this turn) and, 100m/yds further on (just at the start of the woods), turn left. When you come to **transformer building 777**, a little track runs downhill to a fjord-like bay; it's followed in Walk 20. You quickly come to two wide, parallel tracks. Keep to the upper left-hand track, curling uphill through woods. Just past a first hilltop villa, turn off right on a steep narrow path running between two properties (there are **light blue arrows** pointing in the

The walk runs through this small wood, close to the sea

opposite direction). This descent is quite steep and potentially dangerous in wet weather: go carefully! Once down at **Cala Mastella**, head northwest on the small path to the Sa Sení Restaurant, 200m/yds inland from the beach. You are now in the valley of the **Torrent Socarrat**.

From the restaurant continue in the same direction (west) along the asphalt lane but, after 170m/yds, turn right on a dirt track (the second turn-off right you come to). A wall is to your left. When the **wall turns left**, keep straight ahead (northwest) on a path. You descend to cross the Socarrat and rises up the other side. Beyond a villa (La Calma) you come to a track (somewhat under **2h**). Turn left uphill here. (Walk 20 follows this track downhill to Cala Mastella). The streambed is now on your left, and you pass a **pumping station**.

When you come to a **transformer pylon** with the number 1039 you cross the Socarrat again and follow the track uphill to the ridge. Suddenly, in the middle of this wilderness, a **tennis court** pops up on the right! At the T-junction past the tennis court go right, and at the T-junction 100m/yds further on, go left. From here you can look out through the trees to Es Figueral and Cala de Sant Vicent. Two minutes past the junction there's a pretty estate on the right in the valley.

Climbing steeply to the pass between **Puig des Molí** and **Puig de Cap Gros**, ignore all turn-offs right and left. Finally the pretty white church at your destination shines out in the valley, and you come into **Sant Carles** (**2h45min**). Watch out for traffic when you meet the asphalt road in front of Anita's Bar (once the haunt of hippies, now a focal point for the local well-to-do).

Cycle tour 4: ES CANAR • SANT CARLES • ES FIGUERAL • S'AIGUA BLANCA • PUIG D'ATZARO • CAN CODOLAR • ES CANAR

See touring map; see also the walking maps on pages 95 (for the start and end) and 104 (the section north of Sant Carles)

Distance: 20km/12.5mi; 2h

Grade: easy, with ascents of about 200m/650ft overall

Equipment: picnic, water; see also page 14

How to get there and return: cycle circuit based on Es Canar

This circuit mostly follows asphalt country roads with very little traffic. Allow a whole day, even though you will only cover 20km.

Leave **Es Canar** by heading northwest on the road. At a roundabout near Las Delicias you meet the PM810; follow it right to **Sant Carles** (be sure to visit the old church and Anita's Bar). Continue on the PM810 for another 1.5km, then follow signposting down to the right, to **Es Figueral** with its pleasant beach. From there follow a good dirt track northwest along the coast as far as **S'Aigua Blanca**. Now head uphill to the PM810, turn left and ride as far as the next crossroads.

Leave the main road here and turn right towards Sant Llorenç (signposted). This beautiful asphalt lane takes you across a fertile plain, eventually between **Puig d'Atzaró** and **Sa Torreta**. Leave the lane after about 4.5km, turning left before Can Vincent Ribes on a lane signposted to Can Codolar, Es Canar and Santa Eulària, with Puig d'Atzaró (219m) on your right. Cross the PM810 south of **Can Codolar** and continue south and then east, back to **Es Canar** (20km).

One of the island's beautiful old threshing floors lies en route.

Cycle tour 5: ES CANAR • SANT CARLES • CALA BOIX • CALA MASTELLA • SANT CARLES • PERALTA • ES CANAR

See touring map; the start and end of the tour are shown on the walking map on page 95; the section north of Sant Carles on page 104, and the Cala Boix area on page 109.

Distance: 25km/16mi; 3h

Grade: easy, with overall ascents of 200m/650ft

Equipment: picnic, water; see also page 14

How to get there and return: cycle circuit based on Es Canar

Like Cycle tour 3, this 25km round trip follows asphalt lanes with little traffic. Most of the cars you meet are hire cars driven by tourists. But I think you'll agree with me that wherever asphalt lanes make walking not much fun, you'll enjoy the landscape far more on a bike than from a car. You ride much more slowly than in a car, you're perched higher up, so you can see more, and — best of all — you enjoy the wonderful feeling of physical exercise in fresh air.

Leave **Es Canar** the same way as for Cycle tour 3: head northwest on the road. After a little over 1km turn right (northeast) to **Pla de s'Argentara** and soon join the road to Sant Carles that comes from Cala Llenya/Can Jordi. Follow this left to **Sant Carles**, then go north a short way on the PM810 — to the pass between **Puig d'en Gat** and **Puig des Moli**.

At the Y-fork, turn right (northeast) and follow the road towards Es Figueral. After 1.5km turn right to down to **Cala Boix**. From here take the lane near the coast to the restaurant Sa Sení at **Cala Mastella**. After a break, continue on the lane to the main road into Can Jordi, then turn right, back uphill to **Sant Carles**.

From Sant Carles head southwest on the PM810 to the **roundabout**, then turn left back to **Es Canar** (25km).

The pretty church at Sant Carles

Walk 20: CIRCUIT FROM SANT CARLES TO CALA MASTELLA

Distance: 8km/5mi; 3h

Grade: easy, but you must be sure-footed on the coastal rocks; overall ascents/descents of about 300m/1000ft

Equipment: lightweight walking boots or stout shoes with good soles, water, swimwear; see also page 10 (top)

How to get there and return: 🚌 to/from Sant Carles

You follow beautiful woodland trails to Cala Mastella, once a small fishing port. It has a beach. Then you walk over coastal rocks and through a wood to the northern part of Can Jordi. Take a mid-day break here, before heading back to Sant Carles through woods and cultivation.

Start out at **bus stop** by the **parish church** in **Sant Carles** (drawing opposite). Follow the main road uphill for just 40m/yds, to **Anita's Bar**. Then turn right (east) 10m/yds past the bar, on a track waymarked with blue triangles (the track is surfaced initially). Ignore all turn-offs left and right. Almond, carob and fig trees thrive on the cultivated terraces lining both sides of the track. Then the track heads into the woods, and you rise to the **pass between Puig des Molí and Puig des Cap Gros**. There's a right turn here to a private estate and, on the left, a beautiful villa with a swimming pool. Follow the dirt track downhill through the woods, ignoring the left-hand fork behind the villa. At a junction by a **ruined stone house** (three-four minutes down from the pass), turn right; 100m/yds further on, go left on a field track. You pass a **tennis court** on your left, which looks terribly out of place in this isolated wood!

Four minutes past the tennis court, by a **transformer pylon** with the number 1039 and the name 'Socarrat', turn left. You cross the valley of the **Torrent Socarrat**. On the far side of the streambed there's an old house with a **pumping station**. (Walk 19 ascends this track from Cala Mastella.) Soon you come to a new villa in the middle of the woods. Before the villa, turn right on a beautiful track; it curls steeply through the wood down into the valley.

In front of the next property (on the right) a path runs down into the streambed (waymarked with two track-side rocks); follow it. It will take you to the setting shown on page 101, where there are some 40 **impressive pillars**. They're over 100 years old; this was once

99

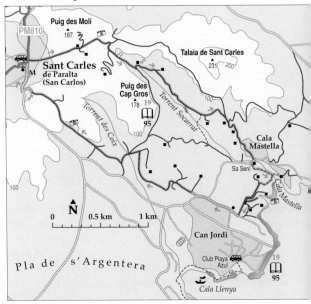

a vineyard. Wooden planks were laid across the pillars, and trellises for the vines were hung from the planks.

After you've inspected the pillars, climb back to the woodland track (**50min**) and continue the walk. Three minutes later you come to a fork. Take the track to the left. Straight away you pass an exceptionally beautiful house on the right built in traditional Ibicenco style, with a roof garden and swimming pool. On the far side of the valley you can see the asphalt road down to Cala Mastella. You cross a low rise, where a track comes in from the left. On the right there's a beautiful house (Can Ribes). Go through a side valley and up to a second rise. Now Cala Mastella is just opposite you. You pass another villa, Can Inshallah.

Turn right to the **Sa Seni** restaurant, walk round it, and take the little footpath along the right-hand side of the valley, down to **Cala Mastella** (**1h**). Nowadays some of the buildings have been taken over by hippies. Some 50m/yds before the beach you pass an old waterwheel well. If you want to swim, watch out for the jellyfish!

Now take the narrow footpath uphill to the right (marked with light blue arrows and green/white paint). On the first part of this coastal path you have to be sure-footed, and sometimes you will need to use your hands.

The word 'Llenya' is written in light blue paint. Follow these waymarks, although the Cala Llenya is not your destination. A branch-off to the left says 'stop' — warning you not to stray onto private property. The well-marked path contours through a wood. Soon you're walking between two private properties, with a wall on your right and a fence on your left. When you come to the iron gate of the property to the right, you'll encounter two private, parallel lanes. Keep to the lane on the right. Both lanes make a bend to the right.

Then you come to a transformer building with the number 777. From here you can take a short stroll down to a tiny fjord-like bay with a beach — but you have to return the same way to the transformer building, as the coastal path south of the little fjord is private. From the transformer house head uphill on a track, past the property Can Lita. At the next T-junction, turn right again on a small asphalt road.

Now you walk northwest — your main direction for the rest of the walk. You pass a **threshing floor** on the right and then a small road off to the left (Walk 19 comes from Can Jordi on this road en route to Cala Mastella.) After another 300m/yds, ignore a lane (Camí Dom Miquel Pere) off to the right. Then, 100m/yds further on, the road you are on curves left. Keep *straight ahead* (northwest) here, with woods on your left and cultivation on your right. The asphalt soon ends. Follow the main track in a bend to the left and then a curve round to the right. At a T-junction, turn left. After about 100m/yds, ignore two turnings to the right and cross the **Torrent des Coix** (**2h**). At the next junction, turn right (about 150m/yds short of the main road).

The author in the bed of the Torrent des Socarrat; this was once a vineyard.

Almonds are harvested in August around Sant Carles.

Now heading northwest again, you walk through cultivation and past *fincas,* with the asphalt road from Cala Llenya to Sant Carles running about 200m/yds over to your left. Eventually you come to a high point and begin your descent to Sant Carles.

The last part of the walk, down to Sant Carles, is asphalted. Don't miss a visit to the old, 17th-century *finca* Ca Andreu, now a museum (**M** on the map). Then continue down to **Sant Carles (3h)**, where you can visit the lovely church shown on page 98 and call in at Anita's Bar — once a hippy hangout, now a watering hole for affluent locals.

Walk 21: SANT CARLES TO CALA DE SANT VICENT

See also photo opposite   **Distance:** 11km/6.8mi; 3h30min

Grade: fairly strenuous, with an ascent of about 200m/650ft and descent of 300m/1000ft; all waymarked with dark blue triangles

Equipment: lightweight walking boots, long trousers, swimwear, picnic, water; see also page 10 (top)

How to get there: 🚌 to Sant Carles
To return: 🚌 from Cala de Sant Vicent

Shorter walk: Follow the main walk and turn back any time you like.

This walk crosses the high Serra de Sant Vicent ridge in the north of Ibiza on one of the few still-viable trails. As you walk through cultivation and isolated woods, there are a lot of forks — so it is very handy to have blue waymarks to follow!

Begin at **bus stop** by the **parish church** in **Sant Carles** (drawing on page 98). Opposite the church is a **bank**, where you head downhill (west-northwest) on an asphalt lane, with banana plantations, orchards of carob and almond trees, and lovely little gardens bursting with vegetables. Ignore a track to the right where the road bends sharp left but, when the road curves left after another 200m/yds (**20min**), turn right on a wide track. Ignore the fork to the left immediately. Continue along this track, ignoring a fork to the right, as you skirt the west side of **Puig d'en Gat**. (See Walk 22 if you want to help find the beehives!) You descend to an asphalt road (**30min**). Follow this 300m/yds to

You pass this typical whitewashed well early in the walk.

the right (to where it bends right). Here take a good farm track straight ahead, northeast. There is fencing on both sides and, off to the right, the bright **white well** shown on page 103. The chain of high hills where you are heading rises beyond this intensively-cultivated valley dotted with *fincas*. Keep straight along this track for about 500m/yds, until you reach a T-junction. Turn right here (southeast) for a good 200m/yds. Then turn

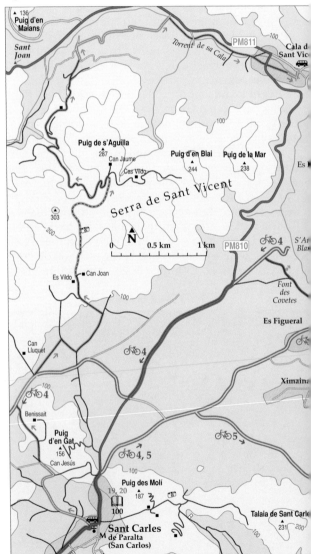

sharp left (northeast) on another track. Again, follow this straight ahead for about 500m, until you reach field track off left. There is a **dark blue triangle waymark on the wall** here.

This marks the **start of your route to the ridge** (**1h**). Start to rise up, at first heading northwest, then north. Beyond a property on the left the track turns right (**1h10min**) towards Can Joan. Leave the track here to **begin the climb proper**: turn half left on a path marked with blue arrows, heading up through pines. At first the path is somewhat faint; keep a **wall** a few metres/yards to your right. Then the path turns away from the wall and is easily followed. Climbing constantly, you quickly gain height. Soon there are fine views down to Es Figueral and Santa Eulària, before you reach the **pass** (**1h40min**)

Descending from the pass, turn sharp left on a wide motorable track (**1h50min**) coming in from the east (from the beautiful Cas Vildo property). The track curves down the left-hand side of the valley. Even this steep valley is intensively cultivated with olive, walnut and carob trees. Then the cultivated terraces come to an end, and the track enters woodland. A few minutes later, ignore a steep track coming in from the left. Two minutes further on, the track crosses the streambed and starts to rise. Ignore a track coming in from the right; shortly afterwards, there's a drystone wall on your right. You pass a very beautiful **old property** three minutes later. Down left in the valley you see Sant Vicent's church, and already cars can be heard on the PM811. Another track comes in from the right and, a few minutes later, your farm track joins an **asphalt lane** (**2h35min**). Follow this to the left downhill for 200m/ yds, then turn right (east). Now keep on this asphalt lane for a good half-hour, curving through the valley (you pass a beautiful tall pine about 20 minutes along).

Some 50m/yds before the PM811, turn right on a signposted farm track, following the bed of the **Torrent de sa Cala**. But soon leave the streambed, heading right on another farm track. After crossing an asphalt lane you walk parallel with the PM811. At a fork, keep left, following the **pale blue-painted metal poles**. A track comes down from the hillside and joins your track. Soon you go under the bridge carrying the Sant Vicent/Sant Joan road. An asphalt lane comes underfoot, and you quickly reach the beach at **Cala de**

Walk 22: ROUND PUIG D'EN GAT

Distance: 9km/5.6mi; 3h

Grade: quite easy, except for a steep climb up a rough path about halfway through the walk; ascent/descent of about 200m/650ft

Equipment: lightweight walking boots, picnic, water; see also page 10 (top)

How to get there and return: 🚌 or 🚗 to/from Sant Carles

Alternative walk: If you're a bit adventurous, you can explore the paths on Puig d'en Gat (see map) for the old Arabic beehives. Some of the woodland paths are partly overgrown, so wear long trousers!

The mysterious pillars in the Socarrat Valley (see photograph on page 101) puzzled me decades ago, when I first discovered them and wrote about them in the first edition of this book. Before long, readers of Ibiza's local newspaper told me what they were. This walk presented me with another puzzle when I first did it years ago; I came upon several sarcophagus-like structures in the woods around Puig d'en Gat. A friend on the island solved this mystery for me, but now the problem is finding them again, and I have to admit failure on my last visit…

Whether you find them or not, it's a lovely walk, partly through woods. You'll also cross cultivated areas, where you'll see many of the island's typical fruits and flowers (even bananas, something of a rarity on Ibiza). And if you're lucky, you'll find the old Arabic beehives on the hillsides of Puig d'en Gat. These beehives are several hundred years old and are slowly disappearing from the landscape — or enclosed in private land.

We start off as in Walk 21. **Begin** at **bus stop** by the **parish church** in **Sant Carles** (drawing on page 98). Opposite the church is a **bank**, where you head downhill (west-northwest) on an asphalt lane, with banana plantations, orchards of carob and almond trees, and lovely little gardens bursting with vegetables. Ignore a track to the right where the road bends sharp left. After another 200m/yds the road curves left (**20min**). Walk 21 turns off right here on a wide track, but for this walk keep to the lane, heading east. Then the land bends right (northwest) and comes to a crossroads with an asphalt country road.

Go straight across and follow a motorable track on the far side, heading northwest in a dead-straight line. Soon you pass transformer house No 3. Carry on until the track ends (**1h**), then head northeast uphill on a footpath, keeping to the left of a fence. The path follows an old wall, and the last part of the climb is a bit of a huff and puff. But soon the path runs into a wide track leading to a villa nearby on the left. Follow the track (surfaced at first) down to the right, enjoying a good view to the coast at Es Figueral. As the track winds southeast, you will pass an old threshing floor on your left. Then you reach the county road you crossed earlier. Follow it to the left (hardly any traffic; it's a great cycling route) for 500m/yds, to a crossing track.

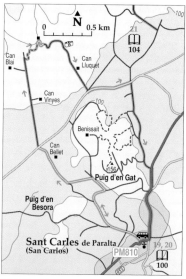

Turn right and follow this track south, past some beautifully planted fields (ignoring two turn-offs right to farms) until you reach the PM810. Then walk *(carefully!)* south on this main road for the last 700m, back to **Sant Carles (3h)**.

Arabic beehives on Puig d'en Gat. A tube of wood inserted into the beehives encouraged the bees to build their combs as they did in trees in the wild.

Walk 23: CALA MASTELLA • TORRE D'EN VALLS • CALA MASTELLA

Distance: 8km/5mi; 2h45min   **Grade:** easy

Equipment: lightweight walking boots, swimwear, picnic, water; see also page 10 (top)

How to get there and return: 🚌 to/from Sant Carles and taxi to/from Cala Mastella, or 🚗 car (park at the Sa Sení restaurant).

Shorter walk: Follow the main walk as far as the scramble over rocks (25min), then return the same way (2.5km/1.5mi; 50min; easy).

Alternative walk: Combine this with Walk 19: see the introductory paragraph on page 94.

O n this walk, you come to the only beach on the island with dark sand, **Cala Boix**. Later another pretty bay, Canal d'en Martí, invites you to swim before — or after — you visit the old watchtower shown opposite.

Begin the walk at the **Sa Sení** restaurant at **Cala Mastella**. Walk down the right-hand side of the valley, past an old waterwheel well, to the beach. First take the narrow, rocky concrete path at the edge of the sea to the fish restaurant, then follow the wide motorable track uphill. Pass a villa, Tres Amigos (with a mock watchtower), and come to an asphalt lane (**10min**).

Follow this to the right, enjoying fine views to Es Canar from this cliff-side road where there are many lovely picnic places (**15min**; Picnic 23). You will follow this lane all the way to Cala Boix because the coastal path in this area has become too eroded through disuse. Sometimes you can take little detours off to the right on small paths to the edge of the cliffs, but you always have to come back to the lane — which is also the route of Cycle tour 5. After passing Casa Cuco the lane forks by **Casa Yasbus**: keep right, down to the large parking area at **Cala Boix** (**50min**). There are a couple of bar/restaurants above the beach. Descend to the bay, where you can swim.

After climbing back up, ignore the track off east to Cap Roig; it's just a cul-de-sac to a private villa. Head inland on the lane behind the Cala Boix Restaurant, then take the first right turn by a drystone wall. There should be a red-painted metal pole here, where the track runs beside the wall. After 200m/yds you come to another red-painted pole at a **three-way junction**: follow the red-waymarked route here: take the middle path which crosses a streambed and passes a **water tank** on the right. On the left you can see Cala de Sant Vicent. After some 250m/yds you meet a track (still the red-

108

waymarked route), where you turn right. There is a drystone wall on your right and fig trees on your left. A further 200m/yds brings you to the asphalt road with the Pou des Lleó restaurant. Follow this road a short way to the right, to a lovely bay with boathouses, **Canal d'en Martí**.

From this bay rise up on a path through dwarf pines and head up to the right, to join a track which runs through a beautiful wood (still the red-waymarked

View through almond trees to the Torre d'en Valls

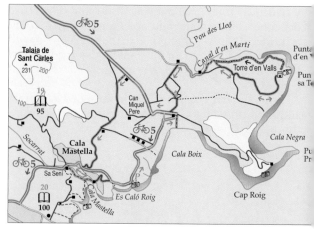

route). Ignore a track off right after 250m/yds. Stone walls support the cultivated terraces here. The gravel track ends at the 18th-century **Torre d'en Valls** (**1h25min**). Over the cliff-edge you look down on Tago Mago.

Experts who don't want to walk back the same way can descend north from the tower. Having reached the coast, you can follow a very narrow coastal path west until you pick up the walk again at Canal d'en Martí. But it is easiest to go back the same way, back down through the beautiful wood. Three minutes after leaving the wood, fork right on the path back down to the sea. Follow the coastal path back to **Canal d'en Martí**, where you could have lunch at the Salado Restaurant and take another swim.

Then walk back to the **Pou des Lleó** restaurant and turn back left on the waymarked farm track After 170m/yds the track bends 90° left between drystone walls, but the waymarked route goes straight on before turning left on the path and passing the water tank. Back at the **three-way junction**, continue to the asphalt lane behind the Cala Boix Restaurant. Turn right here and follow this lane for some 800m/0.5mi, then turn left on a path behind house number 32. The path takes you to a motorable track (Camí a Pou d'es Lleó) where you turn left. Leaving the large **Can Miquel Pere** area off to your left, follow this track southwest through woodland, ignoring all turnings left and right. The track rejoins the main asphalt lane just east of the **Sa Sení** restaurant at **Cala Mastella** (**2h45min**).

PICNIC SUGGESTIONS

1a Es Soto *(plan pages 22-23, photograph page 34)*
Follow Walk 1 to D'Alt Vila and past the Residencia Militar to this undulating area with rocks or grass to sit on (under **40min**). *There are lovely view to the old town and the coast; ample shade.*

1b Beach below Botafoc lighthouse *(map pages 36-37)*
Follow Walk 1 (page 32) from the promenade in Eivissa to this little beach (under **40min**). Return by ⛴ or 🚌 from the Hotel El Corso. *Good swimming, but no shade.*

1c Illa Grossa *(map pages 36-37)*
⛴, 🚌 or 🚗 to/from Talamanca. Pick up Walk 1 at the Botafoc Marina (page 34) and follow it to the highest point on Illa Grossa (about **30min**). *Picnic near the old wartime foundations, with fine coastal views; some shade from bushes and trees. Take care near the unprotected cliffs.*

2a Talamanca *(map pages 36-37)*
⛴, 🚌 or 🚗 to Talamanca, then follow Walk 2 (page 35). Picnic anywhere on this lovely beach — from the start near the Bar Flotante to the eastern end (**10-20min**). *This beach has not changed over the years; you can picnic in full sun, or under the trees at the far eastern end.*

2b Cap Martinet *(map pages 36-37, photograph page 35); **only for sure-footed walkers!***
⛴, 🚌 or 🚗 to Talamanca, then follow Walk 2 (page 35) down to the wonderful coastal rocks (about **45min**). *Unfortunately, you cannot get down to the sea for a swim, and there is no shade.*

2c Cove east of Cap Martinet *(map pages 36-37)*
⛴, 🚌 or 🚗 to Talamanca, then follow Walk 2 (page 35) for about **1h**. You come to a lovely, isolated cove, that can only be reached on foot or from the sea. *Good swimming; shade nearby.*

Cycle tour 1 Salt d'en Serra *(map pages 36-37, photograph page 113)*
⛴, 🚌, 🚗 (Car tour 2) or 🚲 (Cycle tour 1) to Cala Llonga. From Cala Llonga walk or cycle to Salt d'en Serra (**15-20min**). This is an unfrequented pebble beach, sometimes strewn with seaweed. There's a small (seasonal) restaurant nearby. *Good swimming and shade. If you are a strong swimmer, you can swim over to the pretty coves below Puig d'en Vic — they lie just south along the coast.*

Playa Salinas (Picnic 3c), Ibiza's longest and most famous beach

3a Torre de sa Sal Rossa *(map page 43)*

🚐 or 🚗 (Car tour 1) to Platja d'en Bossa. Follow Walk 3 (page 42) for **10-15min** to this old watchtower. *Shade and good swimming.*

3b The rocky coast *(map page 43, similar photograph page 45)*

🚐 or 🚗 (Car tour 1) to Platja d'en Bossa. Follow Walk 3 (page 42) for **50min** to a lonely coastal landscape. *Good swimming, and plenty of shade from pines.*

3c Platja de Migjorn *(map page 43, photograph page 111)*

🚐 or 🚗 (Car tour 1) to Platja de Migjorn (also called Playa Salinas). Walk for a **few minutes** along this long sandy beach, with *good swimming and plenty of shade from pines.*

3d Sa Canal *(map page 43, photographs pages 45, 46, 47)*

🚐 or 🚗 (Car tour 1) to the Can Macià restaurant at Platja de Migjorn (also called Playa Salinas). Walk past the old salt-loading place and some boathouses, with the sea on your left. Then follow the coastal path for **15min**. *Plenty of shady picnic spots under pines; good swimming.*

6 View to Es Vedrà *(map page 52, photographs pages 50-51, 52)*

🚗 (Car tour 1) to Ca na Verguera. Follow Walk 6 (page 50) for **10min**, then find a pretty spot *in the shade of dwarf pines*, with a view out to Es Vedrà.

7 Sa Talaiassa *(map pages 54-55, nearby photograph page 56)*

🚐 or 🚗 (Car tour 1) to Sant Josep. Follow Walk 7 (page 53) for up to **1h15min**. Before you reach the summit of Sa Talaiassa (487m/ 1600ft), you enjoy superb views. *Shade nearby.*

9a Punta sa Torre *(map page 63, photographs on page 62 and below)*

🚐 or 🚗 (Car tour 3) to Portinatx. Follow Walk 9 (page 62) for **45min** — as far as the huge rocks. *Great outlook and good swimming; shade nearby.*

9b Cala Xarraca *(map page 63, nearby photograph page 65)*

🚐 or 🚗 (Car tour 3) to Cala Xarraca. Alight above the cove and walk down to the beach. Then follow Walk 9 (from the 2h45min-point, page 64) for **15min** — to the boat-houses. *Good swimming; shade nearby.*

10 Cala des Multons *(map page 67, photograph page 67)*

🚐 or 🚗 (Car tour 3) to Port de Sant Miquel. Follow Walk 10 (page 66) for **5min**, to a small cove with *good swimming and ample shade*. There's also a seasonal kiosk.

The coastal path towards Punta sa Torre (Picnic 9a)

*Cala Salt d'en Serra
(Picnic Cycle tour 1)*

11 View to Sa Conillera
(map page 72)

🚐, 🚊 or 🚲 (a detour on Car tour 1) to Cala Bassa. Follow Walk 11 (page 70) for about **20min**, until you have a good view of Sa Conillera and its lighthouse. *Good swimming and shade of pines.*

12 Coast north of Cala Gració *(map page 74; the coast north of the picnic spot is shown on page 75)*

🚐 or 🚲 (a detour on Car tour 1) to Cala Gració. Follow Walk 12 (page 73) from Cala Gració for **15min** or more, to the recreation park, near the desalination plant. *Benches under the trees; you can swim, but the coastal rocks are sharp, so take suitable footwear.*

13 Penya Esbarrada *(map page 76, photographs pages 6-7, 77)*
🚲 (Car tour 3) to Santa Agnès. Follow Walk 13 (page 76) for **40min**, up to the viewpoint over Cap Negret and Ses Margalides island. *Ample shade;* small seasonal restaurant.

14 Riu de Santa Eulària *(map page 80, photograph page 79)*
🚐, 🚊 or 🚲 (Car tour 2) to Santa Eulària. Follow Walk 14 (page 78) for **10min**. Before or after crossing the bridge, you can picnic *in the shade of pines* near the mouth of the river.

16 Punta de s'Aguait *(map page 83)*
🚐, 🚊 or 🚲 (Car tour 2) to Santa Eulària. Follow Walk 16 (page 83) for **35min**. Before the coastal path joins the unsurfaced road, take one of the paths down left to the cliff-edge, high above the sea. *Shade from pines.*

17 Views to Eivissa and the sea *(map pages 84-85)*
🚐, 🚊 or 🚲 (Car tour 2) to Santa Eulària. Follow Walk 17 (page 85) for **11 minutes**. You come to a small rise with a beautiful outlook. *Ample shade.*

18 Santa Eulària's Roman bridge *(map page 90, photograph page 90)*
🚐, 🚊 or 🚲 (Car tour 2) to Santa Eulària. Follow Walk 18 (page 88) for about **15min**, to the Roman bridge. There are park benches here, in the colourful setting of oleanders. *Ample shade.*

23 Es Caló Roig *(map page 109)*
🚲 (detour from Sant Carles on Car tour 2) to Cala Mastella. Follow Walk 23 (page 108) for **15min**. There are fine views from the cliff-edge. *Ample shade.*

FORMENTERA

picnics • cycle tours • walk

Cycle tour 1: ES PUJOLS • SANT FERRAN • SANT FRANCESC • CALA SAONA • CAP DE BARBARIA • ES PUJOLS

See map on reverse of car touring map; see also photographs on pages 123, 127, 128, 130 and cover

Distance: 32km/20mi; 3-4h

Grade: easy, with some ascents (up to 50m/150ft)

Equipment: picnic, water; see also page 14

How to get there and return: cycle tour based on Es Pujols

Although the tour is not very long, allow a full day. Picnic 1 lies en route at Cala Saona, where there is also a seasonal restaurant. There is also the chance for a couple of pleasant short walks.

From Es Pujols make first for **Sant Ferrán** (2km). From there turn right and head west to **Sant Francesc** (5km). At the entrance to the town, turn left (south-southeast), following signposting 'Cala Saona/Cap de Barbaria'. You head through cultivation and grazing land, past villas and gardens; the last part of the stretch takes you under pines. Aromatic fennel grows beside the road, and thyme is in bloom here in early summer. Some 2.5km along, at a crossroads, turn right (west) for Cala Saona. Whizz downhill to **Cala Saona** (10km; Picnic 1). It's ringed by rocks, and the turquoise water is crystal-clear. Leave your bike in the shade at the end of the road and find a good picnic spot, in sun or shade.

After lunch, for a change of pace, try this short walk: go a little further along the coast to the west — to **Costa d'es Bou**. (In high season, when Cala Saona is busy, Costa d'es Bou is a quieter picnic spot.) Here you can take another rest break and either sun yourself on the cliffs or lie under the pines. If you don't make it all the way along the Costa d'es Bou, do at least walk the 1km to **Punta Rasa**, from where there is a wonderful view towards the high hills of Ibiza and the rock islet of Es Vedrà. The chalky plateau stretches before you to the south, to Cap de Barbaria. Those who enjoy solitude can do a longer walk from here along the coastal path.

From Cala Saona ride uphill and turn right (south-southwest) on the main road.* On the **Pla del Rei** you pass to the right of a fenced-off archaeological site with high iron gates.

*Some 1km short of the main road the 2.3km-long Camí d'es Cap heads right (opposite a field with fig trees, enclosed by stone walls). This walkers' trail is suitable for all types of cycles and leads to the main road to Cap de Barbaria. Out of season, when there are few walkers about, you might like to use this route as an alternative.

Come to the lonely lighthouse at the end of **Cap de Barbaria** (20km; cover photograph). Unfortunately you won't be able to swim here; the cliffs are far too steep — as you can see in the photograph below! Instead, enjoy a short walk northeast to the **Torre d'es Garroveret**, or explore the impressive **Cova Foradada** in the steep rock wall at the end of the cape. You don't need a torch to climb down to this cave and walk underground to the viewpoint.

Follow the main road from the cape to **Sant Francesc**. Once past the cemetery, head north and then skirt the **Estany Pudent**, to return to **Es Pujols**.

Cliffs above the Cova Foradada

Cycle tour 2: ES PUJOLS • ES CALO • EL PILAR • FAR DE LA MOLA • ES PUJOLS

See map on reverse of car touring map

Distance: 32km/20mi; 3-4h *without detours*

Grade: moderate, with a steep ascent of almost 200m/650ft

Equipment: picnic, water; see also page 14

How to get there and return: cycle tour based on Es Pujols

On this delightful tour you travel almost the entire length of Formentera. Your goal is the lighthouse on the east coast. No picnic places are especially recommended, but there are restaurants at Es Caló and El Pilar. Some cyclists will find the 3km-long climb beyond Es Caló a bit trying — it's far easier with a mountain bike.

From Es Pujols head up to **Sant Ferrán** (2km) and turn left on the main road to El Pilar. From KM6 to KM9 you have the option of cycling on the old **Camí Antic de la Mola** (signposted; see purple line on the map; Picnic 2) Ignore the right turn for Platja de Migjorn (at KM6.5). At KM9.9 you could take a detour a short way to the right, to the Roman ruins (but they are not all that attractive and are closed off by an ugly iron railing). From the ridge descend to the little resort of **Es Caló** (8.5km), where you can shop.

From Es Caló you have a steep climb of 3km on hairpin bends — to the KM15 marker. Another, more gentle climb takes you to the KM16 marker, but then you've made it to the top — you're really fit! The wood ends on this plateau.

Go through the little village of **El Pilar** (13.5km); its attractive church is shown on page 127. Just over two kilometres further on, you're at the **Far de la Mola** (16km). There's a memorial to Jules Verne at this lighthouse, where the cliffs drop steeply down into the sea (watch your step here).

The return is along the same route. Maybe you'll visit the lovely windmill on the west side of El Pilar, from where two detours (neither on asphalt) are possible.

Detour 1: You can follow the same route as Walk 6 up to the highest point on Formentera. From the west side of El Pilar head up an asphalt lane, using the notes for Walk 6 in the last two paragraphs on page 126. From the high point, follow Walk 6 down to the main road near KM15 (or go back the way you came to El Pilar).

Detour 2: From the west side of the village go north on the Camí de sa Cala, through intensively-farmed land and past the Can Purrisines estate, where the track

climbs into a little wood. A stud farm is passed on the right. On the left, in the Ferrer estate, there's a trig point (133m/435ft). From here go northwest downhill. The track ends at pretty Can Simonette, and you return the same way.

On the return to Es Pujols you can take yet another detour: at KM12.8 (on a hairpin bend) go left to the south coast. Leave the bike by the beach and head southeast past the restaurant Es Copinar. There are many lovely places to sunbathe or swim at this beach.

Landscape on the plateau of La Mola

Cycle tour 3: ES PUJOLS • ES TRUCADORS • LA SAVINA • PORTO SALER • TORRE DE LA GAVINA • CALA SAONA • ES PUJOLS

See map on the reverse of the car touring map; see also photographs pages 115, 128-129

Distance: 30km/20mi; 3h

Grade: easy, with some ascents up to 50m/150ft

Equipment: picnic, water; see also page 14

How to get there and return: cycle tour based on Es Pujols

This is a wonderful tour of through the blindingly-white north of the island and the isolated west coast at Punta de la Gavina. Don't forget your sunglasses! The harsh light at the salt-pans would be almost unbearable without some protection for your eyes. Picnics 3a and 3b lie en route.

From Es Pujols head northwest towards Es Trucadors. When you reach the KM3 roadside marker, you can take a little detour left to see the megalithic remains on the low hill, discovered by an amateur archaeologist in 1978. Then continue northwest on the road between the **Salinas d'en Marroig** (salt-pans) and the **Estany Pudent**. These salt-pans are no longer an economic proposition: they are closed and the whole area has been declared a nature reserve. Some rare birds have colonised the area. To get to **Platja de Llevant** ('Tanga Beach') for Picnic 3b, you could cycle through the salt-pans over the walkways shown on page 123.

Just before the KM5 stone the main road turns left. Turn right here, to continue north on a narrower road which continues out to the end of the point. Leave your bike here and, if the sea is calm, wade across **Es Pas** to Espalmador Island (the last stretch is a swim). There are many splendid places for a picnic on either side of this narrow neck of land (**Es Trucadors**; Picnic 3a).

Cycle back to the salt-pans and, beyond the windmill (**Es Moli d'es Carregedor**), take the first right turn. You'll come to the narrow cycle path running north of the asphalt road along the north bank of the Estany Pudent. At the lock in front of **La Savina**, by a stone building shaped like a tent, turn left on the asphalt road (Via Major). Head towards Sant Francesc but, beyond the **Estany d'es Peix**, turn right to **Porto Saler**. Ride to the end of the asphalt road and then turn northwest on Camí de D'Alt Porto Saler. It's a fairly bumpy ride to the **Torre de la Gavina** (18km).

Go back the same way to the start of the asphalt road.

Above: Cavall d'en Borràs; right: the Molí d'es Carregedor

At the crossroads take the signposted track down to
Cala Saona (20.5km). Relax on the beach, then follow
the asphalt road back via **Sant Francesc** to **Es Pujols**.

Detour: If you're not too tired, try this alternative
route to Sant Francesc via Es Mal Pas (add 5km/3mi).
On the return from Cala Saona, go straight over the
road to Sant Francesc, following the Camí de C'an Parra
downhill. Leave this road at the second bend to the
right; go straight ahead on a track. Keep left at a fork.
You cross the Torrent de S'Alga not far from its mouth.
When you approach the coast, you have a beautiful view
to the Torre d'es Català. You come to an asphalt lane
(by a white mock tower): it takes you north and then
northwest, up towards Sant Francesc. Following the
Camí de Migjorn, you meet the Cap de Barbaria road
just short of Sant Francesc. From here return to Es
Pujols on the main road via Sant Ferrán or the shorter
and more beautiful route from the cemetery which
skirts the Estany Pudent.

Cycle tour 4: ES PUJOLS • PLATJA DE MIGJORN • ES PUJOLS

See map on the reverse of car touring map
Distance: 10km/6.2mi; 1h
Grade: easy, with an ascent of 50m/150ft in each direction
Equipment: picnic, water; see also page 14
How to get there and return: cycle tour based on Es Pujols

This cycle tour takes you to one of the most beautiful beaches on Formentera and is especially recommended during the months when swimming is possible. Take a little rucksack with you, so that you can walk unencumbered as far as far as you like along the beach. Picnic 4 is en route.

From Es Pujols first head up to **Sant Ferrán** (2km), where you turn left (southeast). At about KM6.7 turn right down to the coast. You come to a little holiday resort called **Es Ca Mari**, at the end of the asphalt road. Park your bike in a shady spot and walk barefoot along the beach — go left or right, it doesn't matter…

This is the **Platja de Migjorn**, one of the loveliest beaches on Formentera, and there are any number of delightful picnic spots (Picnic 4). Feel like walking? Heading west, you could walk all the way to the cliffs at the Cap de Barbaria; heading east you should be able to go as far as the resort called Mar y Land.

Return the same way to **Es Pujols**.

Typical landscape with drystone walls

Cycle tour 5: ES PUJOLS • PUNTA DE SA PEDRERA • TORRE DE LA GAVINA • ES PUJOLS

See map on the reverse of car touring map
Distance: 21km/13mi; 2h
Grade: easy, with a few ascents of about 50m/150ft
Equipment: picnic, water; see also page 14
How to get there and return: cycle tour based on Es Pujols

This tour doesn't always follow asphalt roads; sometimes you'll have to dismount. But the landscape is superb — especially in May and June, when the thyme is in flower (as in the photograph on pages 118-119).

From Es Pujols first head southwest along the Camí de S'Estany up to **Sant Francesc**. You meet the main road (Via Major; 3km) by the cemetery; follow it into the village. Then head up past the church to **two windmills** — the Molí Quixote, then a second mill, next to a trig point. Enjoy the panorama from this high point.

Cycling lanes through the salt pans

From here continue northwest on the lane. It meets the lane from La Savina to Porto Saler by a house called La Colina. Turn right, northeast, down to the **Estany d'es Peix**. At Residencia Arenas Doradas turn left on Camí de S'Estany d'es Peix. It runs into Camí de sa Pedrera and takes you via the old **Estanyets salt-pans** to **Punta de sa Pedrera** (10km), where bizarre rocks enclose a small cove (**Caló d'es Moro**). Leave your bike below the trig point and take a short walk, to enjoy these coastal rock formations. Then follow the gravel track southwest to a lonely *finca*, from where a sandy track leads to the Torre de la Gavina. Stop for a swim in the peaceful cove, **Racó d'es Banc**. Then make for the **Torre de la Gavina** (12km), which can be visited.

Now head southeast on dirt tracks to the crossroads where the asphalt lane to La Savina begins. Turn left and retrace the route you took earlier, but continue down to the Via Major. Follow it 300m to the left, turn right at the entrance to **La Savina**, and take the Camí d'es Brolls via the **Estany Pudent** back to **Es Pujols**.

Cycle tour and walk 6: ES PUJOLS •
SANT FERRAN • ES CALO • CAMI DE SA PUJADA •
EL PILAR • SA TALAIASSA • ES CALO •
ES PUJOLS

See map on reverse of car touring map

Distance: 18km/11mi; 2h cycling; 9km/5.6mi; 3h walking

Grade: cycle tour: easy, with 50m of ascents/descents; walk: moderate, with overall ascents/descents of 200m/650ft; you must be sure-footed in a couple of places, where the path nears the cliff-edge.

Equipment: walking boots for the hike, water, picnic (or have lunch at the Hostal Entre Pinos at KM12.3); see also page 14

How to get there and return: cycle tour based on Es Pujols; the walk can also be reached by car or bus.

This is a combination of a cycle tour and a walk, and keen walkers will agree that the hike is the best part of the excursion. Besides the walk described, I have shown other possible routes on the map. For instance, from near KM15 you could walk south to S'Estufador and either return the same way or go west to the Caló d'es Ram and return on the Camí d'es Ram. It helps to have a good sense of direction when following any paths — and it's a good idea to have the latest *Mapa de Formentera* as well (see page 16).

From Es Pujols first head uphill to **Sant Ferrán**. Turn left there and take the cycle path beside the main road to **Es Caló** (8.5km), where you can shop for food and water in summer. Before the road starts to climb, turn left to the **Hostal Entre Pinos** (9km), where you leave your bike.

Begin the walk by heading uphill on the signposted **Camí de sa Pujada** (old name: Camí Romà), signposted as Walk No 16. You pass the Pinomar apartments and some villas. This very old path was resurfaced in 2001 — for the second time (the first time was in 1797, but it wasn't done for tourists then!). As you climb more steeply, you'll spot vestiges of the old cobbled trail. Ignore a fork off left to the sea, pass through a clearing, and come onto a wide woodland track. Ignore another trail off left to the sea; continue straight ahead uphill. Now the trail narrows into a footpath, offering the beautiful view shown opposite down into the **Racó de sa Pujada**. Fine views stay with you — along the whole coast and over to Ibiza. Where the path runs near the cliffs, there are ropes to keep you clear of the edge (see photo overleaf).

Soon you pass a cave on the right of the trail (**Cova de sa Mà Peluda**). Later, the path skirts the wall of a

124

property, where a signpost gives the distances to Es Caló and El Pilar. The trail is asphalted here and turns right, up towards the road.

You can ignore this first turning towards the road, but you cannot avoid joining the road because of private property — so take the second turn-off right, to the **main road**. Follow the road to the left for about

Racó de sa Pujada

100m/yds, crossing a valley. Leave the road at a small transformer building on the far side of the valley, by turning left on a path, heading northwest alongside an old ruined wall. Soon the wall and the path bend to the right, and you now head northeast for a while.

The path becomes vague, but as soon as you have left the wood you see the way ahead very clearly in front of you —as well as an overwhelming coastal landscape. You cross two walls at gaps made for specially for

Where the Camí de sa Pujada runs near the cliff-edge, there are ropes to dissuade you from going too close.

Above: the little church at El Pilar; right: not an abstract painting, but fish drying on the branches of a dead tree

walkers. Then you walk alongside a wall on your left. A few old *fincas* are visible in the distance, and for the next few minutes you head towards them — walking pathless over grass. Then you cross this wall as well, at another purpose-made gap. Now head for the **last wall before the coast**, go through another gap and walk (*carefully*) alongside the cliffs. Just before a house the path is very near the cliff-edge. At this house you cross a knee-high wall and walk to the next house, with the number Monestir 4961.

Now you come onto a wide track and follow it in a south-southeasterly direction, past another *finca* with the letters MHDJ. Turn left at a T-junction; beyond a bend, you again head south, past *fincas* with the numbers 4859 and 4957. Grapevines are growing here, near a two-storey yellow house. To the left, in the distance, you can see the lighthouse (Far de la Mola).

When you come to a crossing, go straight over, taking the small path through the wood, still heading south-southeast. At a T-Junction, turn right, back to the main road — which you join just at the border separating the two districts of Monestir and Talaiassa. Cross the road in **El Pilar** and follow a concrete lane opposite, heading southeast. You pass a soccer pitch and a radio transmitter station.

When you come onto the asphalted **Camí de sa Talaiassa** (Camí No 9), follow it to the right, slowly ascending. This asphalt road soon becomes a track at Casa Montana 2. Follow the track to the right, heading northwest for a short time. But at house No 4813, turn left (southwest). Very soon you come to the house on **Sa Talaiassa**, the highest point on Formentera. You can see the trig point on its upper terrace.

From here follow the track north downhill. The track bends to the right after a while and leads through woods, back to the main road (which you meet close to KM15). You've been on this section of the main road before. Cross the road, turn left, and after just a minute turn right, back onto the Camí de sa Pujada.

Now you could simply retrace your outgoing route back to the Hostal Entre Pinos. But if you are sure-footed, why not vary your return? Turn right after the Racó de sa Pujada and leave the Camí de sa Pujada on a path heading seawards. From a viewpoint on this path you can walk closer to the Racó de sa Pujada and see it from a different angle. From the viewpoint return to the main path and follow it northwest downhill,

between the cliffs and the Camí de sa Pujada. You will need to be sure-footed where this path crosses a valley. The last part of the path, down to Es Caló, is easy. Once at the houses above the bay of S'Enfossol, turn left to the **Hostal Entre Pinos** (**3h**), where you left your bike.

From here cycle back the same way to **Es Pujols**.

PICNIC SUGGESTIONS

Be sure to carry a picnic basket or small rucksack with you when you cycle. There are many lovely picnicking spots on Formentera, where you can spend the whole day. Of course you will take bathing things; cycling is even more enjoyable after a refreshing swim.

Picnic numbers correspond to cycle tour numbers; the cycle tours take you to the picnic spots. A map reference follows the name of the picnic spot: the exact location is indicated on the map of Formentera by the symbol **P**, printed in green. Some picnic places are illustrated.

It goes without saying that you will leave the picnic spot as clean as you found it — even cleaner. If you carry a plastic bag with you, you might even take away rubbish left by someone else. All 'Landscapers' try to set a good example for other nature lovers to follow…

1 Cala Saona *(map on reverse of touring map, photograph overleaf)*
10km/6.2mi; follow the notes for Cycle tour 1, and find a lovely picnic spot, either by the beach or a bit higher up, under the pines.

2 Camí Antic de la Mola *(map on reverse of touring map, photograph pages 118-119)*
up to 6km/4.3mi; follow the notes for Cycle tour 2, but use the

Cavall d'en Borràs, 1km northeast of La Savina

alternative route from KM6. There are some lovely picnic spots on this old track, but only the odd tree for shade.

3a Es Trucadors *(map on reverse of touring map, photograph page 115)*
4km/2.5mi; follow the notes for Cycle tour 3 to the straits of Es Pas (**30min**). You'll find many lovely picnic spots on this neck of land (Es Trucadors), but *no* shade.

3b Tanga Beach *(map on reverse of touring map)*
3km/under 2mi; follow the notes for Cycle tour 3 to the salt-pans (Salinas Marroig). Cross the salt-pans on the walkways shown in the photograph on page 123. Behind the salt-pans lies a beautiful sandy beach. Its official name is Platja de Llevant, but the area is known locally as 'Tanga' ('Bikini') Beach … although the female sun-worshippers here often wear something even skimpier than bikini-bottoms. When you cross one of the pans you'll have to push your bike a short distance.

4 Platja de Migjorn *(map on the reverse of touring map)*
10km/6.2mi; follow Cycle tour 4 to Es Ca Marí and wander along the long beach, Platja de Migjorn, until you find a spot you fancy.

5 Caló d'es Moró *(map on the reverse of touring map)*
12km/7.4mi; follow Cycle tour 4 to this rocky bay on the west side of Punta de sa Pedrera — or go there more directly (about 7km). Picnic above or at the cove; little shade.

6 Camí de sa Pujada *(map on the reverse of touring map, photographs on pages 125, 126)*
9km/5.6mi cycling, then a very short walk. Follow Cycle tour 6 and the start of Walk 6. On the ascent from Es Caló you will find several viewpoints, some with benches. Plenty of shade.

The lovely beach and crystal-clear waters of Cala Saona

BUS AND BOAT TIMETABLES

On the following pages are bus and boat timetables for the destinations given below. The numbers following the place names are *timetable numbers*. Only high season timetables are included here; outside summer, the bus and boat services are less frequent. Note also that these are 'work day' timetables (Mondays to Fridays). There are fewer buses on Saturdays, Sundays and holidays. There are four bus companies on Ibiza. However, they produce a joint timetable, which you should pick up at the bus station in Eivissa when you arrive. Or update the timetables in this book at www.ibizabus.com. *In the left-hand column you'll find the outgoing departure times; the right-hand column lists departures times for the return journey.*

Airport 🚌1
Cala Azul 🚌23
Cala Bassa 🚌13
Cala Codolar 🚌15
Cala Conta (Platjes de Comte) 🚌15
Cala Gració 🚌17
Cala Llenya 🚌23; ⛴29, 33, 42, 43, 44
Cala Llonga 🚌4, 26; ⛴27, 36, 41, 42
Cala Pada ⛴28, 32, 38, 43
Cala de Sant Vicent 🚌6
Cala Tarida 🚌11, 14
Cala Vedella 🚌12
Canar, Es 🚌20; ⛴37, 38, 39, 40, 41
Cap Martinet 🚌9

Cap Negret 🚌17
Figueral, Es 🚌22
Formentera ⛴30, 35, 40, 44
Mola, La 🚌52
Pilar, El 🚌45, 46, 49, 52
Pujols, Es 🚌47, 48, 49
Sant Ferrán 🚌46, 48, 49, 50, 52
Sant Francesc 🚌45, 46, 47, 48, 51
Savina, La 🚌45, 47, 50, 51
Eivissa (Ibiza Town) 🚌1, 2, 3, 4, 5, 6, 7, 8, 9, 10, 11, 12, 16, 18, 19; ⛴27, 28, 29, 30, 31, 34, 39
Jesús 🚌4
Platja d'en Bossa 🚌2

Portinatx 🚌7, 24
Port de Sant Miquel 🚌5
Puig d'en Valls 🚌9
Sant Antoni 🚌10, 13, 14, 15, 16, 17, 18, 19, 21
Sant Carles 🚌22, 23, 25
Sant Jordi 🚌1, 3
Sant Josep 🚌11, 12, 16
Sant Joan 🚌6, 6a, 7, 24
Sant Rafel 🚌18
Santa Eulària 🚌8, 20, 21, 22, 23, 24, 25, 26; ⛴32, 33, 34, 35, 36, 37
Santa Agnès 🚌10, 19
Ses Salines 🚌3
Talamanca 🚌4, 9; ⛴31

1 Eivissa—Sant Jordi—Airport
🚌 Line 10

07.00	07.20

and half-hourly until

23.00	23.50

(in July and August every 15min)

2 Eivissa—Platja d'en Bossa
🚌 Line 14

07.00	07.20

and half-hourly until

23.40	23.40

(every 20min from 1/6 to 30/9)

3 Eivissa—Sant Jordi—Ses Salines
🚌 Line 11

09.30	10.00
10.30	11.00
11.30	12.00
12.30	13.00
13.30	13.00
15.30	16.00
16.30	17.00
17.30	18.00
18.30	19.00
19.30	20.00

4 Eivissa—Talamanca—Jesús—Cala Llonga
🚌 Line 15

09.00	08.30
10.00	09.15
11.00	11.30
12.30	13.00
15.00	13.15
16.00	15.30
17.00	16.30
18.00	17.30
19.30	18.30

5 Eivissa—Port de Sant Miquel
🚌 Line 25A

08.45	09.30
10.15	11.00
13.30	16.15
17.00	17.45
18.30	19.15
20.15	18.00

6 Eivissa—Sant Joan
🚌 Line 20

10.15	09.30
12.40	11.30
17.30	16.45
19.30	18.45

6a Sant Joan—Cala de Sant Vicent
🚌 Line 20B

13.20	08.35
20.10	16.30

7 Eivissa—Sant Joan—Portinatx
🚌 Line 20A

10.15	09.15
12.40	11.15
17.30	16.30
19.30	18.30

8 Eivissa—Santa Eulària
🚌 Line 13

07.30	07.30
08.00	08.00
08.30	08.30
09.00	09.00
09.30	09.30
10.00	10.00
10.30	10.30
11.00	11.00
11.30	11.30
12.00	12.00
12.30	12.30
13.00	13.00
13.30	13.30
14.00	14.00
14.30	14.30
15.00	15.00
15.30	15.30
16.00	16.00
16.30	16.30
17.00	17.00
17.30	17.30
18.30	18.00
19.30	18.30
20.30	19.00
21.30	19.30
22.30	20.00
23.30	20.30
24.30	21.30
and hourly until	
02.00	02.30

9 Eivissa—Puig d'en Valls—Talamanca — Cap Martinet
🚌 Line 12

07.00	07.00
and hourly until	
21.00	21.00

from 1/07 until 31/08 extra buses at

22.00	22.00
23.00	23.00

10 Eivissa—Santa Agnès—Sant Antoni
🚌 Line 30

12.45	09.00
21.00	16.00

11 Eivissa—Sant Josep—Cala Tarida
🚌 Line 38

10.30	09.15
12.30	11.15
20.30	17.15

12 Eivissa—Sant Josep—Cala Vedella
🚌 Line 26

11.00	10.00
13.00	12.00
17.00	18.00
19.00	20.00

13 Sant Antoni—Cala Bassa
🚌 Line 7

09.30	10.00
10.30	11.00
11.30	12.00
12.30	13.00
15.30	16.00
16.30	17.00
17.30	18.00
18.30	19.00

14 Sant Antoni—Cala Tarida
🚌 Line 5

09.15	09.45
10.15	10.45
11.15	11.45
12.15	13.00
15.15	15.55
16.35	17.15
17.45	18.25
19.05	19.45

15 Sant Antoni—Cala Conta—Cala Codolar
🚌 Line 4

09.10	09.40
10.10	10.40
11.25	12.00
12.30	13.10
15.30	16.00
16.30	17.15
18.00	18.45

16 Sant Antoni—Sant Josep—Eivissa
🚌 Line 8

07.00	08.00
and hourly until	
19.00	20.00

17 Sant Antoni—Cala Gració—Cap Negret
🚌 Line 1

09.30	10.00
10.30	11.00
11.30	12.00
12.30	13.00
13.30	13.45
16.30	17.00
17.30	18.00
18.30	19.00
19.30	20.00
20.30	21.00

18 Sant Antoni—Sant Rafel—Eivissa
🚌 Line 3

07.00	07.30
to	to
23.30	23.30

every half hour, (but every 15min between 09.00 and 22.00 Mon-Sat)

**19 Sant Antoni—
Santa Agnès—
Eivissa**
🚌 Line 30

09.00	12.45
16.00	21.00

**20 Santa Eulària—
Es Canar**
🚌 Line 18A

07.45	08.00

and half-hourly until

17.15	17.00

and then as follows

18.00	17.45
18.45	18.30
19.30	19.15
20.15	20.00
21.00	20.45
21.45	21.30
22.30	22.15
	23.00

**21 Santa Eulària—
Sant Antoni**
🚌 Line 19

09.30	10.15
11.00	11.45
12.40	13.15
15.30	16.15
18.00	18.45

**22 Santa Eulària—
Sant Carles—
Es Figueral**
🚌 Line 16B

08.50*	10.25
09.30	09.45*
13.00	13.55
13.30*	15.45*
17.30	18.20
18.00*	18.55*

**23 Santa Eulària—
Sant Carles—
Cala Llenya—
Cala Azul**
🚌 Line 16A

10.15*	09.05
12.30*	10.30*
13.00	12.45*
15.00	15.20
16.15*	16.30*
19.30*	19.45*
20.00	20.20

*Sat only

**24 Santa Eulària—
Sant Joan—
Portinatx**
🚌 Line 21

12.30	09.05
19.15	17.00

**25 Santa Eulària—
Sant Carles**
🚌 Line 16

09.30	09.10
13.00	10.30
15.00	15.25
17.30	18.25
20.00	20.25

**26 Cala Llonga—
Santa Eulària**
🚌 Line 41

08.00	09.00
09.30	10.00
10.30	11.00
11.30	12.00
12.30	13.00
13.15	16.00
15.30	17.00
16.30	18.00
17.30	19.00
18.30	20.00
19.30	
20.15	

**27 Eivissa—Cala
Llonga* ⛴**

11.30	10.45
12.30	11.45
14.30	13.45
15.30	16.45
16.30	
17.30	

* via Santa Eulària

**28 Eivissa—Cala
Pada* ⛴**

12.30	10.00
17.30	15.15

*via Santa Eulària

**29 Eivissa—Cala
Llenya* ⛴**

11.30	08.45
12.30	10.00
16.30	13.00
17.30	15.00

*via Santa Eulària

**30 Eivissa—
Formentera ⛴**

09.15	07.30
09.30	08.30
10.15	10.15
11.00	11.00
12.00	12.30
13.30	16.00
15.15	17.00
17.30	18.00
18.30	18.30
20.00	19.00
20.30	20.00

**31 Eivissa—
Talamanca ⛴**

09.00	09.00
and	and
every	every
half	half
hour	hour
until	until
20.00	20.00

**32 Santa Eulària—
Cala Pada ⛴**

09.30	10.00
13.30	15.15
18.30	18.45

**33 Santa Eulària—
Cala Llenya ⛴**

09.30	08.45
12.30	10.00
13.30	13.00
17.30	15.00
18.30	18.00

**34 Santa Eulària—
Eivissa ⛴**

10.30	11.30
11.30	12.30
12.30	14.30
13.30	15.30
15.30	16.30
16.30	17.30

**35 Santa Eulària—
Formentera ⛴**

09.30*	17.15*
10.30	18.30*

*only 1/5-31/10

36 Santa Eulària—Cala Llonga 🚂

10.30	10.00
11.30	11.00
12.30	12.10
13.30	13.10
15.30	15.10
16.30	16.10
17.30	17.10
18.30	18.00

37 Santa Eulària—Es Canar 🚂

10.30	10.00
11.30	11.00
12.30	12.00
13.30	13.00
15.30	15.00
16.30	16.00
17.30	17.00
18.30	18.00

38 Es Canar—Cala Pada 🚂

10.00	10.00
11.00	11.00
12.00	12.00
13.00	13.00
15.00	15.00
16.00	16.00
17.00	

39 Es Canar—Eivissa 🚂 *

10.00	11.30
11.00	12.30
12.00	14.30
13.00	15.30
15.00	16.30
16.00	17.30

* via Santa Eulària

40 Es Canar—Formentera 🚂

10.00	17.15

41 Es Canar—Cala Llonga 🚂

10.00	10.00
11.00	11.00
12.00	12.00
13.00	13.00
15.00	15.00
16.00	16.00
17.00	17.00
18.00	18.00

42 Cala Llenya—Cala Llonga* 🚂

08.45	09.00
10.00	12.00
13.00	13.00
15.00	17.00
18.00	

* via Santa Eulària

43 Cala Llenya—Cala Pada* 🚂

08.45	09.00
10.00	12.00
13.00	13.00
15.00	17.00
18.00	

* via Santa Eulària

44 Cala Llenya—Formentera 🚂

08.45	17.00

45 El Pilar—Sant Francesc—La Savina 🚌

06.40	12.30*
09.30*	15.00
14.00	17.20
16.00	

* also run on Sat/Sun/public holidays

46 Sant Francesc—Sant Ferrán—El Pilar 🚌

12.30
15.05
18.00

47 Es Pujols—Sant Francesc La Savina 🚌

10.15*	10.45*
16.15	11.30*
17.25*	12.20*
	15.00

* also run on Sat/Sun/public holidays

48 Sant Francesc—Sant Ferrán—Es Pujols 🚌

10.55
11.40
12.30
15.05
18.00

49 Es Pujols—Sant Ferrán—El Pilar 🚌

15.30	09.30
18.10	16.00

50 Sant Ferrán—La Savina 🚌

07.05
10.10
16.25
17.40

51 Sant Francesc—La Savina 🚌

07.05
10.10
16.25
17.40

52 Sant Ferrán—El Pilar—La Mola 🚌

12.40
15.15
18.15

☀ Index

Geographical names comprise the only entries in this index; for other entries see Contents, page 3. A page number in *italic type* indicates a map; a page number in **bold type** a photograph or drawing. Both may be in addition to a text reference on the same page. *All* places in the Formentera index are shown on the map of Formentera on the reverse of the touring map.